THE COMMUNITY COOK BOOK

LECTOR HOUSE PUBLIC DOMAIN WORKS

THE COMMUNITY COOK BOOK

ANONYMOUS

ISBN: 978-93-89614-19-0

Published: -

LECTOR HOUSE LLP
E-MAIL: lectorpublishing@gmail.com

THE COMMUNITY COOK BOOK

A PRACTICAL COOK BOOK, REPRESENTATIVE OF THE BEST COOKERY TO BE FOUND IN ANY OF THE MORE INTELLIGENT AND PROGRESSIVE AMERICAN COMMUNITIES

SOLD BY

CLASS OF WILLING WORKERS
OF THE
WINTER ST. BAPTIST CHURCH HAVERHILL, MASS

THIRD EDITION

1916

IN COMPILING AND REVISING THIS BOOK, ONE PERSON
AND HER NEEDS WERE ALWAYS KEPT IN MIND—THAT
PERSON IS THE AVERAGE AMERICAN WOMAN, AND
TO HER THIS BOOK IS DEDICATED IN THE FIRM BELIEF
THAT IN IT SHE WILL FIND MUCH HELPFULNESS.

FOREWORD

The Community Cook Book is a collection of recipes chosen from many hundreds that may well be considered representative of the best to be found in any of the more intelligent and progressive of American Communities in which a part of the population make occasional visits to all parts of the country from which they bring back choice recipes to contribute to the neighborhood fund. Added to this, that constant change and interchange of a part of the population, and if the best recipes of such a section be carefully selected and classified, then in a real American Community's Cook Book, such as this, we have one of the most valuable practical cook books in the world.

In presenting this cook book, the compilers were guided by the fact that what each housekeeper needs, is not so much a great variety of ways, but a few successful ways of preparing each article of food.

CONTENTS

BREAD, BISCUITS, ROLLS AND PASTRY

"'Bread,' says he, 'dear brothers, is the staff of life.'"

BAKING POWDER BISCUITS.

Two cups flour, two teaspoonfuls baking powder, one-half teaspoonful salt, two tablespoonfuls lard, a little sugar if desired, one-half cup milk or water, milk preferred. Mix flour, salt, sugar and baking powder well with fork; add milk. When well mixed, drop in small quantities onto buttered pans. Bake eight minutes in moderate oven.

BAKING POWDER BISCUITS.

Two cups flour, two teaspoonfuls baking powder, one-half teaspoonful salt, two tablespoonfuls butter, milk enough to make soft dough. Mix dry ingredients, chop in butter, add milk, mixing all the while with a wooden paddle or knife. Toss on a small floured board, roll lightly to one-half inch in thickness. Shape with cutter. Place on a buttered pan and bake in a hot oven.

BOSTON BROWN BREAD.

One level pint cornmeal scalded, one level tablespoonful salt, one cup New Orleans molasses, two teaspoonfuls soda over which pour a little boiling water, one pint sour milk; put half the soda in the molasses and the remainder in the milk. Stiffen with Graham flour. Steam four hours, and brown in oven for about fifteen minutes.

BUCKWHEAT CAKES.

One cake yeast, one coffee-cup cornmeal, two coffee-cups buckwheat, one teaspoonful salt, one quart tepid water. Before cooking, add four tablespoonfuls milk and two of molasses in which you have stirred a teaspoonful of soda.

CORNBREAD.

Sift three-fourths cup cornmeal, three-fourths cup flour, two and one-half teaspoonfuls baking powder, three-fourths teaspoonful salt, one tablespoonful sugar. Work in tablespoonful butter, then add three-fourths cup sweet milk, into which one or two eggs have been beaten. Pour into greased pans and bake in a moderate oven. If sour milk is used, take one and one-half teaspoonful baking powder and one-fourth teaspoonful soda.

CORN GEMS.

Two eggs, one-half cup white flour, one cup milk, one cup corn flour, one tablespoonful butter, one teaspoonful salt, one heaping teaspoonful baking powder. Pour enough boiling water over corn flour to wet it and burst starch grains. Beat eggs very light. Mix dry ingredients to corn flour, then eggs, milk and last butter. Bake twenty-five minutes in hot oven.

CRUMPETS.

One pint of milk, four ounces butter, one teaspoonful salt, one cake compressed yeast, three cups flour. Scald milk and let stand until lukewarm, then add salt and flour, beat vigorously, then add butter melted and the yeast, beat again, cover and stand in a warm place until very light. Grease muffin rings and place them on a hot griddle. Fill each ring half full of batter. Bake until brown on one side, then turn and brown the other side. Take from the fire and stand aside until wanted. When ready to use, steam and serve with butter, marmalade, syrup, jam, or anything else desired.

DUMPLINGS.

One pint flour, one level teaspoonful salt, one heaping teaspoonful baking powder, one heaping teaspoonful lard, enough milk and water to make a soft dough. Roll one-half inch thick, cut in squares, or with biscuit cutter, and lay in on top of stew. Cook ten minutes.

FRENCH BREAD.

After softening one cake of compressed yeast in one-half cup lukewarm water, stir in enough flour to make a very stiff dough. Knead well, shaping into a ball. Make two cuts on top about one-quarter inch deep. Place in a pan of tepid water until it swells and floats. When very light put into a bowl containing one-half cup salted water, stir in enough flour to make a stiff dough. Let stand in a temperature of 68 or 70 degrees F. until light. Shape into loaf, let lighten again and bake.

GRAHAM BREAD.

Two cups sour milk, two teaspoonfuls soda dissolved in little warm water, one-fourth cup sugar, one-half cup molasses, one egg, salt, three and one-half cups Graham flour. Bake one hour.

GRAHAM BREAD.

With one pint warm milk, one cake of yeast and white flour, make a sponge. One teaspoonful salt not heaped, one-half cup molasses. Let rise, then stir in sifted brown flour till partly stiff, put in baking pan, let rise, then bake.

GRIDDLE CAKES.

One-half pint milk, one-half pint warm water, one-half cake yeast, one teaspoonful salt, one egg, one tablespoonful melted lard, flour enough to make a batter like ordinary batter-cakes. Let rise over night and fry for breakfast.

KENTUCKY CORN BREAD.

One pint thick, sour milk, two teaspoonfuls salt, one egg. Mix with this enough cornmeal to make a batter not stiff. Use meal of medium fineness—not the very fine sold in most groceries. Beat well; add last one level teaspoonful soda dissolved in a little water. Allow a tablespoonful of lard to become very hot in baking pan; pour into the batter, stir, and turn into pan. Bake until cooked through.

MILK BREAD.

Scald one pint of milk, pour while hot over a tablespoonful of butter, one tablespoonful sugar, one teaspoonful salt. When nearly cold, add one-fourth cake of yeast, dissolved in one-half a cup of lukewarm water, add flour stiff enough to knead. Knead until smooth and elastic, cover, and let rise until morning, then shape into loaves, let rise again, bake from forty to fifty minutes; rolls from fifteen to twenty minutes.

MUFFINS.

One egg, one-half cup sugar, two cups flour, two heaping teaspoonfuls baking powder, three-fourths cup milk, salt. Mix egg with sugar. Sift flour, baking powder and salt, add to egg and sugar alternately with the milk and beat well. In season add blueberries. If short of milk, use part water.

NUT BREAD.

Four and one-half cups wheat flour, eight teaspoonfuls baking powder, one teaspoonful salt, one cup sugar, two cups sweet milk, one large cup chopped walnuts, two eggs well beaten. Stir all dry ingredients together thoroughly, add eggs and milk. Stand twenty minutes before baking. Bake in two tins about forty-five minutes in a moderate oven.

PARKER HOUSE ROLLS.

Two cups scalded milk, two tablespoonfuls sugar, one teaspoonful salt, two tablespoonfuls butter, one egg, one yeast cake dissolved in one-fourth cup lukewarm water. Mix dry ingredients and butter in the hot milk; when slightly cool, add flour enough to make a drop batter, beat well, add the yolk of egg, then the white beaten until stiff, and lastly the dissolved yeast cake, beat hard. Then add flour enough for a soft dough that you can handle. Turn on a well-floured board and knead until covered with blisters, turn into a well-buttered bowl. Cover and place in a temperature of 75 degrees until it doubles its bulk. Shape into rolls, butter and cover until they are very light. Bake in a quick oven until a delicate brown.

PARKER HOUSE CORN ROLLS.

One and one-fourth cup white flour (measurements level), three-fourths cup cornmeal, four teaspoonfuls baking powder, one-half teaspoonful salt, one tablespoonful sugar, two tablespoonfuls butter, one egg, one-half cup milk. Method: Mix and sift dry ingredients in a bowl; chop butter in with a knife; beat egg, to which add one-half cup milk; add all slowly to dry ingredients to make a soft dough that can be handled; add more milk, if necessary; toss lightly on floured board and pat to one-half inch thickness; cut with round cutter, patting piece of butter in center; fold in center, so that opposite edges meet; put in buttered baking sheet; wet top with milk and bake in quick oven ten to fifteen minutes.

POP-OVERS.

Two cups milk, one cup flour, two eggs, one-half teaspoonful salt. Beat eggs very light with Dover egg beater, add flour, milk and salt. Warm muffin pans slightly, butter them, and fill half full. Bake in hot oven until brown. This will make twelve pop-overs.

POTATO ROLLS.

Two cups hot mashed potatoes (four cups of sliced potatoes make about two cups of mashed potatoes), one scant cup lard, two tablespoonfuls of sugar, two teaspoonfuls salt, three well-beaten eggs. Mix all well together and have it luke-warm, then add one-half cake of yeast, which has been soaked in a cup of luke-warm water for twenty minutes. Let rise two hours in a warm place; work up (not too stiff) with flour; rise again. When very light, roll thin on a biscuit-board, cut with a cutter, put in pan, rise again, and bake in a very hot oven. This will make about sixty rolls.

REQUESTED BROWN BREAD.

Two cups each of Graham flour, cornmeal and buttermilk or sour milk, two-thirds cup of New Orleans molasses, two and one-half teaspoonfuls soda and a little salt; steam three hours; soda in sour milk.

SALLY LUNN.

Mix one pint of flour, two teaspoonfuls baking powder, one-half teaspoonful salt, yolks of two eggs well beaten, one-half cup milk, one-half cup butter melted, whites of two eggs beaten stiff. Bake in muffin pans or drop loaf fifteen to twenty minutes. If for tea, add two tablespoonfuls sugar to flour.

SODA BISCUIT.

Mix well one teaspoonful salt, one-half teaspoonful soda, two and one-half cups flour. Mix thoroughly with one heaping tablespoonful lard. Pour in one cup thick, sour milk or buttermilk; stir up quickly, adding as much flour as may be necessary to make stiff enough to handle. Roll about one-half inch thick. Bake in hot oven.

SPOON BREAD.

Make a pint of cornmeal mush, five eggs, salt, tablespoonful of butter. Stir butter and salt into mush when warm; let cool, then add eggs, a cup of milk and two teaspoonfuls of baking powder. Bake. Serve with a spoon from baking dish.

WAFFLES.

Mix one pint flour, two level teaspoonfuls baking powder and one-half teaspoon salt. Add one and one-fourth cup milk, three well-beaten egg yolks, two tablespoonfuls melted butter and the whites of the three eggs, beaten stiff. Grease the hot waffle iron and put in the batter. Cook about one minute, then turn the iron and cook a little longer on the other side. Serve immediately with butter and maple syrup or marmalade.

SANDWICHES.

Philadelphia cream cheese, chives. Cut chives into small pieces with scissors. Mix into the cheese and spread on rye bread.

One-half pound boiled ham, two dill pickles, one teaspoonful mustard. Grind ham and pickles in a meat chopper, mix in mustard, and spread on white or rye bread.

Ten cents' worth peanuts, one cup mayonnaise. Grind peanuts in a meat chopper and mix with dressing. Spread on white bread, with a lettuce leaf in each sandwich.

One cake Eagle cheese, one ten-cent can pimentos. Mix half of this quantity at a time. Grind or chop the pimentos very fine, mix well with cheese, and spread on rye bread.

One can sardines, one-half cup mayonnaise. Mash sardines in a bowl, mix with dressing, add salt, pepper and a little lemon juice. Spread on rye or white bread.

WALNUT-RAISIN SANDWICHES.

Grind English walnuts and raisins and put in a few drops of hot water to make them thin enough to spread on reception flakes.

PIES AND PASTRY

PASTRY.

One cup sifted flour, one-half cup lard (cut lard into flour with knife), one-fourth teaspoonful salt. Ice water to form stiff dough.

APPLE PIE.

Pare, core and cut five sour apples into eighths; place evenly in a pie plate lined with the usual pie pastry. Mix one-third cup sugar, one-fourth teaspoonful grated nutmeg, one-third teaspoonful salt, teaspoonful lemon juice and a few gratings of lemon rind and sprinkle over apples. Dot over with little lumps of butter, wet edges of under crust, cover with upper crust and press edges together. Bake forty-five minutes in a moderate oven.

JAM PIE.

One cup of raspberry or blackberry jam, yolk of two eggs, one cup rich milk or cream, one tablespoonful flour; mix thoroughly, cook over fire until thick. Use the whites of egg for meringue. Bake with bottom crust.

LEMON CUSTARD PIE.

One cup sugar, three eggs, one cup milk, one tablespoonful flour, three tablespoonfuls powdered sugar, juice and rind of one lemon. Beat yolks of eggs and sugar; add juice and rind of lemon. Mix flour with the milk, and pour through sieve into eggs and sugar. Line a deep pie plate with good rich paste; pour in the mixture and bake in a quick oven thirty minutes. Beat whites of eggs to a stiff froth and add three tablespoonfuls powdered sugar, beating all the while. Put on top of pie, and return to oven until a light brown.

LEMON PIE.

One cup water, one cup sugar, one lemon, two eggs, one tablespoonful butter, one heaping tablespoonful flour. Bake crust on the outside of pan, first pricking with a fork. Boil sugar and water; add to the beaten yolks of eggs the grated peel of lemon, butter and flour; pour over this the boiling mixture, then boil until it thickens like custard. Cool, turn into baked crust, spread on top whites of eggs beaten stiff, to which add a tablespoonful pulverized sugar. Place in oven until the meringue is brown.

MOCK CHERRY PIE.

One cup cranberries cut in half, one-half cup chopped raisins, one cup sugar, one tablespoonful flour, a pinch of salt, one teaspoonful vanilla and one-half cup boiling water. Bake with upper and under crust.

PUMPKIN PIE.

Peel and cut up in squares, cook with half pint of water, one cup sugar, one-fourth teaspoonful red pepper, boil slowly till soft and perfectly dry, then sift; two beaten eggs, one-half cup sugar, three and one-half large spoonfuls pumpkin, one-half cup milk, small pinch of salt, one-fourth teaspoonful cinnamon, a little more of ginger. Makes one pie. Bake slowly one hour.

SHORTCAKE.

Three cups flour, two teaspoonfuls baking powder, one-half teaspoonful salt; sift three times; one-half cup butter mixed with flour till like meal. Beat one egg light, add to it a cup of cold water. Mix with flour. Put in two pie pans, or in muffin pans for individual shortcakes, and sprinkle tops with granulated sugar. When baked, split, butter and put sweetened berries between, and garnish tops with sweetened whipped cream and whole berries.

WAFERS.

Cream one-third cup butter, add one cup powdered sugar. Mix well. Add one-half cup milk alternately with two scant cups flour, or enough to make a stiff batter. Spread very thin on a slightly greased tin. Bake in very slow oven until light brown. Remove from oven and place on top of stove. Cut and roll in desired shape. These wafers can be flavored with ginger, sprinkled with chopped nuts or filled with whipped cream and berries.

CEREALS, BREAKFAST FOODS

"Look up! the wide extended plain
Is billowy with its ripened grain,
And on the summer winds are rolled
Its waves of emerald and gold."

CORN MEAL MUSH.

Allow one pint of meal and one teaspoonful of salt to a quart of water. Sprinkle meal gradually into boiling salted water, stirring all the time. Boil rapidly for a few minutes, then let simmer for a long time. Very palatable served with milk; some people like it with butter and pepper. For fried mush let it get cold, then cut in slices, dip in flour and fry in suet until brown.

HOMINY.

This is very good when well cooked, and may be simply boiled until done in salted water, and served with pepper and butter. It is good fried like mush.

MACARONI WITH CHEESE.

After boiling macaroni in salted water until soft, sprinkle with grated cheese; repeat, pour over a sauce made of butter, flour, salt and scalded milk; cover with bread crumbs and bake until brown.

RICE.

Rice has been cultivated from time immemorial. While not so valuable a food as some of the other cereals, it forms the larger part of the diet of people in the tropics and in semi-tropical countries, and is used extensively in other places. It is eaten by more human beings than any other cereal; is not equal to wheat as a brain food, but worthy of the high place it holds in the estimation of mankind.

It may be simply boiled and served as a vegetable, with pepper and butter, or served with sugar and cream. It is good cooked in milk. Is baked like macaroni with cheese, and cooked in various ways in combination with meat or vegetables.

BOILED RICE.

One of the quickest ways of preparing rice is to fill a large kettle with water, allow it to come to a boil; when bubbling vigorously throw in two cups of rice and boil hard twenty-five minutes. Empty into a colander and dash under cold water, which will separate the grains. Season with pepper and salt, heap lightly on a dish and put a lump of butter on top.

ROLLED OATS.

None of the breakfast foods which are so much used are so wholesome as a simple dish of rolled oats or the old-fashioned oatmeal. Served with or without cream and sugar, these are to be highly recommended to persons who are compelled to live indoors a great deal, and are generally relished by those who lead an outdoor life. Although rolled oats is supposed to be a dish quickly prepared, it is better, like oatmeal, for being cooked a long time, and baked for two hours, after being boiled a few minutes, it is very palatable and nutritious.

SOUPS

"La soupe fait le soldat." ("The soup makes the soldier.")

BEAN SOUP.

One pint navy beans, soak over night, cook till they are very tender, add some celery and little tomato, salt and pepper to taste, cook all well together. In another saucepan let boil one tablespoonful of butter, add a chopped onion, fry till it is clear. Mix a tablespoonful of flour with a cup of the soup and a little butter, cook a moment or two, add to soup and let all boil ten minutes, add a pinch of red pepper and strain.

BOUILLON.

Twenty-cent beef soup bone, ten-cent knuckle of veal, twenty cents' worth chicken gizzards, seven quarts cold water. After reaching boiling point add one small handful salt; three or four whole peppers, one carrot, one onion, one celery root, one turnip, one parsley root, one bay leaf, two or three whole allspice, one-half can tomatoes. Let boil slowly one day. Strain and skim.

BOUILLON.

Chicken bones, three pounds beef, three quarts water, four whole cloves, one onion, one carrot, two pounds marrow bones, four peppercorns, a bouquet of herbs and one bay leaf, three stalks of celery, juice of a lemon, two tablespoonfuls butter or marrow, one-half cup of sherry, one turnip. Put vegetables in last, spices about one-half hour; brown vegetables in butter or suet; brown a few pieces of meat, to give a good color to the soup, turn into soup digester and cover with cold water. Let it come to a boil, skim, and let it simmer; cover and cook for five hours. Strain in an earthen vessel, cool, remove fat, clear and serve hot in cups.

CORN SOUP.

One can cornlet or corn, one pint cold water, one quart heated milk, two table-spoonfuls butter, one tablespoonful chopped onion, two tablespoonfuls flour, two teaspoonfuls salt, one-fourth teaspoonful white pepper, yolks of two eggs. Chop corn, cook it with the water twenty minutes; melt butter, add chopped onions and cook until light brown; add flour, and when thoroughly mixed add milk gradual-ly. Add this mixture to corn and season with salt, pepper, rub through sieve, heat again. Beat yolk of eggs, put them in soup tureen, and pour soup over them very slowly. When mixed serve immediately.

CREAM OF CELERY SOUP.

A pint of milk, a tablespoonful of flour, one of butter, a head of celery, a large slice of onion and a small piece of mace, a little salt. Boil celery in one pint of water from thirty to forty-five minutes; boil mace, onion and milk together; mix flour with two tablespoonfuls of cold milk. Cook ten minutes. Mash celery in water it has been cooked in and stir in boiling milk. Strain and serve.

CREAM OF CORN SOUP.

Put one pint of milk in a double boiler, add one pint of grated corn, two teaspoonfuls of salt; rub together one tablespoonful of flour and one of butter. Add them to the soup when boiling. Just before serving add one-half pint of whipped cream.

FRENCH PEA SOUP.

Cover a quart of peas with water and boil with an onion till they mash easily. Mash and add a pint of water. Cook together two tablespoonfuls each of flour and butter until smooth but not brown. Add to the peas with one pint of cream and a cup of milk. Season with salt and pepper, strain and serve.

MIXED VEGETABLE SOUP.

Fifteen-cent soup bone, three quarts water, half a small cabbage cut very fine, three large potatoes, two good-sized carrots, two turnips, one medium-sized onion, three teaspoonfuls salt, one-half teaspoonful pepper, a little celery and green pepper. Put on in cold water with all vegetables except potatoes. Cook very slowly one hour. Do not cover closely. At the end of one hour add potatoes and cook an hour longer. Put in two or three tomatoes when potatoes are added, if liked.

MOCK BISQUE.

One-half can tomatoes strained, one quart milk, one-third cup butter, one tablespoonful cornstarch, one teaspoonful salt, one salt-spoon pepper, heat milk in double boiler. Mix smoothly one tablespoonful butter, cornstarch and seasoning, add hot milk slowly. Boil ten minutes and add remainder of butter and strained tomatoes. Serve immediately.

MUTTON BROTH.

Remove pink skin from mutton, also fat; have the meat from the neck. Cover well with water, let boil slowly, cook until meat becomes ragged. One tablespoonful rice.

OYSTER SOUP.

Put about fifty oysters in a colander and drain. Pour over them a pitcher of cold water, and then put them into a hot kettle. Let stand covered for a few minutes. Add one pint of water. Rub together a tablespoonful of butter and one of flour; add a little of the soup to make a smooth paste. Put this with a quart of milk into the soup kettle with oysters, and stir till it begins to thicken. Add a teaspoonful of salt, and pepper to taste.

POTATO SOUP.

To one gallon of water add six large potatoes chopped fine, one teacupful rice, butter the size of an egg, one tablespoonful flour. Work butter and flour together and add one teacupful sweet cream just before taking from the fire. Boil one hour.

TOMATO BOUILLON.

One quart tomatoes, one tablespoonful onion minced, one tablespoonful parsley minced, one tablespoonful lean ham minced, one tablespoonful butter, one pint water, six whole peppercorns, four whole cloves, one bay leaf, salt-spoon paprika, one egg, one tablespoonful sugar. When the whole mixture has thoroughly boiled, add sugar and salt to taste; brown the onion and parsley in the butter, add to the other ingredients; boil all ten minutes, then strain and cool; when perfectly cold stir in the white of one egg, then beat thoroughly with Dover beater, place on stove and stir constantly (to prevent egg from cooking) until the mixture comes to a boil. Stand a few minutes on the back of the stove, strain very carefully through a sieve covered with a cheese-cloth wrung out in hot water. Serve hot. This will serve five persons.

TOMATO SOUP.

To one quart of tomatoes add one pint of water, one tablespoonful sugar, one teaspoonful salt, six cloves and a little pepper; let boil ten minutes. In another saucepan put one tablespoonful butter. When it boils, add a chopped onion and some parsley, and let fry about five minutes, then add one tablespoonful flour previously mixed with water; boil all for ten minutes, strain and serve.

VEAL BOUILLON.

Two knuckles of veal, four quarts of cold water, one onion, one stock celery, one bay leaf, twelve cloves, one teaspoonful salt, one blade mace, one pinch pepper. Put veal in soup kettle with cold water and salt. Simmer gently four hours. Cut up the vegetables and add with spices and simmer one hour longer. Strain, cool, remove fat, reheat and serve with teaspoonful whipped cream on each cup.

FISH

"Fools lade water, and wise men catch the fish."

BAKED WHITE FISH.

Clean and prepare the fish. Make a stuffing of one cupful of cracker crumbs, one teaspoonful chopped parsley, one teaspoonful chopped onion, two table-spoonfuls chopped suet or bacon or one large tablespoonful butter, one-third tea-spoonful salt, two teaspoonfuls chopped pickles, one-quarter teaspoonful pepper. If a moist stuffing is desired, add one-quarter cup milk. Bake fifteen minutes to a pound, allowing ten or fifteen minutes if the fish is unusually large.

CODFISH BALLS.

Boil and mash as many potatoes as desired, using about one-half pound of soaked and drained codfish to a pound of potatoes. Have fish picked apart, and af-ter soaking and drying mix thoroughly with potatoes, adding, for one-half pound of codfish, one tablespoonful butter, yolks of two eggs, one-half teaspoonful salt and a dash of pepper. Make into balls, dip in beaten egg and bread crumbs and fry in hot fat.

FINNAN HADDIE.

Boil a three-pound haddock until the skin comes off easily, remove every par-ticle of bone, cut into small pieces, shred; put one-half pint cream into a chafing dish, add three finely-chopped hard-boiled eggs, rub together two rounded table-spoonfuls flour and two of butter, add to the other ingredients. Now light the lamp under the chafing dish. Stir until the mixture begins to thicken, then blend a raw yolk and add it to the haddie. Sprinkle with finely-chopped parsley and serve on toast. Should there not be quite enough sauce, sweet cream may be added.

FRIED FISH.

Brook trout, perch, catfish and other well-known fish are good fried. Cook in lard, suet or oil. Wash and clean, wipe dry, dip in beaten egg and roll in bread crumbs. Fry in oil, if possible.

FRIED OYSTERS.

One pint large oysters, one-half cup flour, one-half cup milk, one-half tea-spoonful salt, one-half cup fresh tomato catsup. Mix thoroughly the flour, milk, catsup and salt; dip oysters into mixture, then roll in cracker crumbs. Fry in sweet, fresh lard until a dark brown. Serve very hot.

HOLLANDAISE SAUCE.

Rub one-half cup butter to a cream, add the yolks of two eggs, one at a time, then salt and cayenne pepper. About five minutes before serving add one-half cup boiling water. Thicken in double boiler. Add lemon juice.

LOBSTER A LA BUSHMAN.

Cut the meat of four-pound lobster into large pieces; melt one tablespoonful butter and one teaspoonful minced onion, let cook until yellow. Add the lobster, salt, cayenne pepper, two tablespoonfuls white wine; simmer for five minutes, then sprinkle one tablespoonful flour over this. When well mixed, add six or eight mushrooms cut fine, one tablespoonful chili sauce, add one cup water or stock. Cook five minutes longer in shells, put a mushroom on each, sprinkle with buttered cracker crumbs. Bake till brown.

OYSTER COCKTAIL.

Mix one tablespoonful tomato catsup, one-half tablespoonful vinegar or lemon, two drops Tabasco sauce, one-half teaspoonful salt, one teaspoonful finely chopped celery and one-half teaspoonful Worcestershire sauce. Chill these ingredients thoroughly, pour over eight oysters and serve in cocktail glasses.

OYSTER NEWBURG.

One pint oysters, one-half cup cream, one teaspoonful onion juice, two tablespoonfuls butter, one-half teaspoonful salt, one-eighth teaspoonful paprika, two level tablespoonfuls flour, one teaspoonful lemon juice, yolk of one egg, toasted bread. Melt one tablespoonful butter, add oysters, salt, paprika, onion and lemon juice, cook three minutes, and melt remaining tablespoonful butter, add flour, and when blended add cream, then the yolk of the egg, beaten slightly; cook until it thickens, stirring slowly, add to the oysters, mix and serve on toast.

OYSTER OMELET.

Make a plain omelet, beat six eggs until light, separately; add two tablespoonfuls milk, one of flour, one-fifth teaspoonful baking powder, put in flour and rub with milk, salt to taste. Fry in melted butter in a hot skillet. Put in oven for a few minutes to brown on top. Turn out on a good-sized meat dish, pour upon it the oyster sauce and serve at once, hot.

SAUCE.

Make the oyster sauce first. Take twenty-five large oysters, put them in a saucepan over a moderate fire, and cook slowly until the gills are curled. Drain, save the liquor, add enough milk to make a pint. Take a tablespoonful flour and one of butter and cream them. Put the liquor in a pan and when it begins to boil stir in the flour and butter. Stir until boiling, add a teaspoonful salt and a dash of paprika. Stand in a warm place until you make the omelet.

OYSTER PATTIES.

Cook one heaping tablespoonful flour in one heaping tablespoonful butter; add slowly one cup hot milk, season with one teaspoonful salt, one-fourth teaspoonful red pepper; wash over one pint oysters, parboil until plump, skin carefully, drain and add the sauce, fill the patty shells when ready to serve.

OYSTER TENDERLOINS.

Take out one dozen oysters for the gravy first; then take one pint of oysters (pour off most of the liquor and save to put in the gravy); one pint of cracker crumbs rolled but not fine, pepper and salt to taste; also add a pinch of sage to the crumbs. Roll the oysters in the crumbs and put in butter the size of an egg. Cut the tenderloins in the center, roll until flat, then sew together, making a pocket. Stuff with the oysters and sew up the end. Put butter the size of an egg in a pan and brown. Pour this on top of the tenderloin, sprinkle over it salt, pepper and flour. Roast in a moderate oven one and one-half hour. To make the gravy, pour in the liquor and a little water and thickening. Drop in the oysters a few minutes before taking off the stove.

SALMON LOAF.

One can salmon. Drain off juice into stewpan, place salmon in a pan and add one-half cup fine cracker crumbs, two eggs, salt and pepper. Mix thoroughly, press into a mold, steam one hour.

DRESSING.

One and one-half cup milk, four tablespoonfuls catsup, piece of butter size of an egg; boil; thicken with one tablespoonful cornstarch dissolved in water. Pour over loaf when done.

SALMON ON TOAST.

Toast bread and butter it. One and one-half pint milk and cream mixed; heat boiling hot; two tablespoonfuls flour, three tablespoonfuls butter. Work butter and flour together at boiling point, stir this in the milk. Strain salmon in colander upon top of stove, to get warm; then put on toast and pour cream dressing over all. Take three hard-boiled eggs and grate the yellows on top of salmon, and slice the white of eggs around edges of toast in the platter.

SALT MACKEREL IN CREAM.

Wash the mackerel and soak over night in clear, cold water. Lay in a baking pan, and to one mackerel add one-half pint of new milk; put into a moderate oven and bake one-half hour. Just before the fish is done, drop a few pieces of butter onto it.

SCALLOPED OYSTERS.

Roll the crackers, line the baking dish with butter; put the oysters, with a few cloves, salt and pepper, in a stewpan for say five minutes, but do not let them boil. Put a layer of oysters in the baking dish, then a layer of crackers, and so on, having the crackers on top. Bake twenty minutes.

SALADS

"Salads and eggs and lighter fare."

More progressive Americans now understand the value of the salad, and in this way use many vegetables, fish and meats that heretofore have not been extensively used for that purpose. There is room for much interesting experimenting in the making of salads. Almost endless variety may be had by ingenious mixing and combining of suitable ingredients. Used sparingly, they give a zest to the plainest meal, and the olive oil which is used so frequently in the preparation of salads is of immense value in promoting health.

The greens used in making salad, lettuce, dandelion and water cress should always be most carefully washed, and served only when fresh, crisp and cold. Many canned vegetables and left-overs may be used in salad, which would not be nearly so appetizing prepared in any other way.

ASPARAGUS SALAD.

Use either fresh or canned asparagus. If fresh, of course it should be cooked in the usual way and allowed to cool. Only very tender asparagus is suitable for salad. Cut green or red peppers into rings, put four stalks in each ring. Place these bundles on lettuce leaves and serve with usual French dressing. A little pat of Philadelphia cream cheese may be put on edge of each plate.

BEET RELISH.

One quart chopped beets, one quart chopped cabbage, one cup ground horseradish, one cup brown sugar, salt and pepper to taste. Pour over enough vinegar to moisten well about three cups. Heat and seal.

BOILED DRESSING.

Four tablespoonfuls vinegar, one tablespoonful butter, one-half tablespoonful sugar, yolks of three eggs, one cup whipped cream when ready to serve. Boil vinegar and sugar, turn on beaten yolks of eggs. Return to fire, and when as thick as boiled custard remove and add butter.

COLD SLAW.

One-half cup vinegar boiled, two teaspoonfuls sugar, one-half teaspoonful salt and mustard, one-half teaspoonful pepper, one-quarter cup butter to a cream, one teaspoonful flour; pour into boiling vinegar, cook five minutes. One well-beaten egg, with the cabbage chopped fine; pour vinegar over while hot.

COMBINATION SALAD.

Line a dish with lettuce. Arrange on it a layer of sliced tomatoes, thin layer of chopped onions, one sliced cucumber and one green pepper chopped fine. Pour over these layers a dressing made as follows:

Beat yolks of two eggs; add slowly about one cup of olive oil, beating all the time, two tablespoonfuls vinegar, salt and pepper to taste.

COOKED SALAD DRESSING.

One teaspoonful salt, one teaspoonful mustard, one and one-half teaspoonful sugar, few grains cayenne, three-fourths tablespoonful flour, yolks of two eggs, three-fourths cup of scalded milk, one-half cup hot vinegar, one and one-half teaspoonful melted butter. Mix the dry ingredients, add the yolks and mix thoroughly; add the scalded milk, return to double boiler, add the hot vinegar, stirring constantly until mixture thickens, add the butter. Cool before using.

FRENCH DRESSING.

One saltspoonful salt, one-half saltspoonful white pepper, three tablespoonfuls olive oil, one-half teaspoonful onion juice, one tablespoonful vinegar. Mix in order slowly. One spoonful lemon juice may be used in place of onion juice.

FRUIT SALAD.

Bananas sliced lengthwise in quarters; over this put pineapple in cubes. Boil the pineapple a few minutes, to make it more tender. Then large strawberries and English walnuts. Over it put a spoonful of mayonnaise. Make the mayonnaise as you would a filling for lemon pie, with two lemons. Add whipped cream to it before serving.

HOT SLAW.

Chop or slice one medium-sized cabbage; put in boiling water, well covered; boil fifteen minutes, drain off all water and add a dressing made as follows: Half teacup vinegar, two-thirds as much sugar, salt, pepper, one-half teaspoonful mustard, one tablespoonful butter or olive oil. When this is boiling hot add one teacup cream and one egg, stirred together; mix thoroughly and immediately with the cabbage. Cook a moment. Serve hot.

LETTUCE SALAD.

Remove the outer leaves from a large, solid head of lettuce. Tear each leaf into three or four pieces; put them into a towel and on ice or in a cold place. When wishing to serve, put into a bowl, mix one tablespoonful vinegar, one-half teaspoonful salt and one-quarter teaspoonful pepper and sprinkle over the lettuce; stir well, add four tablespoonfuls thick, sweet cream and mix quickly. Serve at once.

MAYONNAISE.

Two tablespoonfuls butter, one teaspoonful mustard, one teaspoonful salt, four teaspoonfuls sugar, one-half cup vinegar, one cup cream, yolks of four eggs. Beat yolks together, add butter, mustard, salt and sugar. Boil cream and add to mixture. Boil vinegar and add. Then put on fire and stir until it thickens.

MAYONNAISE.

Yolks of eight eggs, two tablespoonfuls butter, one cup sugar, one tablespoonful flour, one teaspoonful salt, one teaspoonful mustard, one and one-half cup strong vinegar, two-thirds cup water. Mix flour, mustard and sugar together; add to it the beaten eggs, sugar and butter; then add vinegar and water, and cook over slow fire, stirring all the time. Thin with cream when ready to use, and add celery seed if desired. One-half of this can be made at one time.

NEW ENGLAND POTATO SALAD.

One pint of cream, yolks of two eggs, one-half teaspoonful dry mustard, one-half teaspoonful salt, one-half teaspoonful pepper. Beat yolks for a few minutes, add mustard, salt and pepper, then mix with the cream and put in double boiler; let come to a boil. Put pepper and salt (more, if deemed necessary) and vinegar over potatoes or cabbage about ten minutes before putting in the dressing.

POTATO SALAD.

Boil six good-sized potatoes in their jackets. When cold, peel and put in chopping bowl; add two medium-sized onions, two hard-boiled eggs and chop fine. Add dressing.

DRESSING.

Two eggs well beaten, one cup sweet milk. Boil milk and eggs until it thickens, then add one tablespoonful sugar and butter size of walnut. One-half cup vinegar; salt and pepper to taste.

SALAD NO. 1.

Put alternate slices of tomatoes and pineapple on lettuce leaves and put a large spoonful mayonnaise over each.

SALAD NO. 2.

Chop celery, English walnuts and apples, mix with mayonnaise. Serve on lettuce leaves.

SALAD.

Use lemon Jello as directed on the box. When beginning to get livery, put in thin slices of stuffed olives and pour in small cup to mold. Turn out on lettuce leaves and put a spoonful of mayonnaise on each.

SOUR CREAM POTATO SALAD.

Slice thin cold boiled potatoes and salt well, pour over thick sour cream and stir gently, cut celery in small pieces and mix; let stand one hour, then put in vinegar and stir, using one-third as much as cream. Let stand in cool place two or three hours.

SWEDISH SALAD.

One cup each of boiled potatoes, beet root, fish (mackerel, salmon or cold meat), celery root or stock, one apple, all cut up in small squares; chop some olives and pickles very fine, salt and pepper to taste. Mix in enough cream to make it stick together. Make a sauce by lightly whipping some cream and adding vinegar. Garnish with hard-boiled eggs, olives and beets.

SWEETBREAD SALAD.

One pair sweetbreads, two cucumbers, one cup mayonnaise. Decorate with shredded lettuce border.

SWEET CREAM DRESSING.

Mix together two tablespoonfuls olive oil, one teaspoonful salt, two tablespoonfuls sugar, two tablespoonfuls vinegar. Then add one-half cup tomato catsup and one cupful sweet cream, beating in gradually. This dressing is good for fish, as well as vegetable salads.

TOMATO-CUCUMBER SALAD.

Take nice shaped tomatoes, remove skin, scoop out the seed, sprinkle with salt and put in cool place. Cut cucumbers in bits, fill the tomatoes and serve with whipped cream, lemon juice, salt and pepper.

TOMATO SALAD.

Cut the tomatoes half or two-thirds size if desired. Take out the inside and cut into dice. Fill the shells with ice. One cup tomatoes, one-half teaspoonful shredded onion. Over this pour mayonnaise dressing made with one egg, well-beaten oil, pour in until a little thick, salt, pepper and vinegar. Have all very cold. One teaspoonful of this dressing to a cup of tomatoes. Serve in the tomato shells. Nasturtium leaves are pretty on the plate to garnish.

MEAT

"Meat was made for mouths."

While it is undoubtedly true that raw meat is, as a rule, more easily digested than cooked, our present state of civilization demands that it be cooked, and we can only comply with the demand, preparing the food in question so that it may be not only attractive to the eye, but in a manner that will render it pleasing to the taste and readily assimilated. Cooking softens the tissues, making the act of eating more enjoyable, and also destroys parasitic growths.

To boil meat when broth is not desired, plunge into boiling water. The water should be allowed to boil for about ten minutes and then be permitted to fall somewhat below boiling point and kept at even heat for a long time. The juices and flavors are thus retained.

It is not desirable that fish should be treated in this manner, as the boiling water would break it into little pieces.

To stew meat, put small portions into cold water and raise temperature slowly, until very hot, but not quite boiling. Let it remain thus for some hours, and a rich broth, as well as juicy and tender meat, will result.

In roasting meat it is well to remember that the smaller roast requires the hotter fire. Intense heat produces a semi-solid condition of the exterior, and prevents the drying up of the meat juices. Great heat would be inapplicable to large cuts, the exterior of which would be burned to a coal under such treatment before the heat could reach the interior.

Young housekeepers and others who are not familiar with the various cuts of meat obtainable in most of our markets will do well to consider thoughtfully the accompanying illustrations.

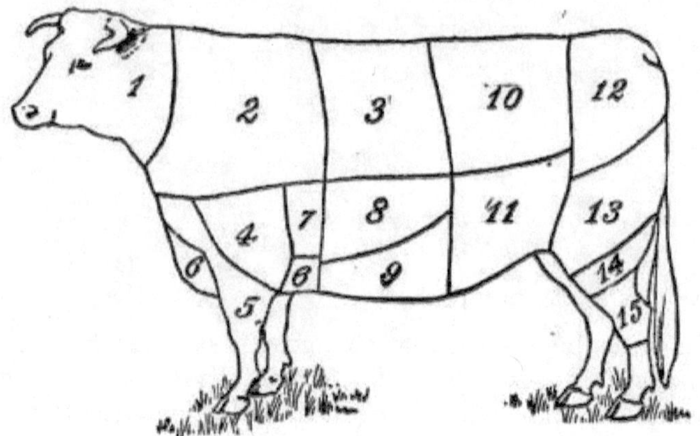

1. Neck. 2. Chuck. 3. Ribs. 4. Shoulder clod5. Fore shank. 6. Brisket. 7. Cross ribs.8. Plate. 9. Navel. 10. Loin. 11. Flank12. Rump. 13. Round. 14. Second cut round. 15. Hind shank.

FIG. 1.—Diagrams of cuts of beef.

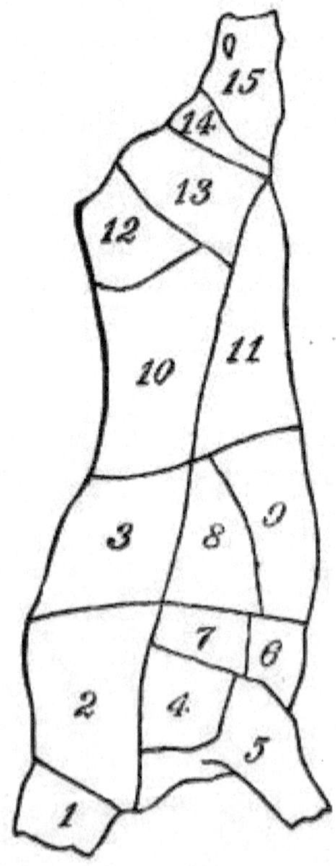

In selecting beef we must remember that color is of great importance. The surface of a fresh lean cut should be a bright red, while the fat should be clear white. After being exposed to a warm atmosphere the surface will of course become darker in color.

The loin commands a higher market price than any other cut, on account of its tenderness and quality. The names applied to different parts of the loin vary in different localities. The part nearest the ribs is often called the "short steak," the other end the "sirloin."

It is interesting in this connection to recall the story which has been told regarding the origin of the word "sirloin." It is said that this steak found such favor with some epicurean king of olden times that he, in a spirit of jocularity and good humor, bestowed upon it the honor of knighthood, to the great delight of his assembled court, and as "Sir Loin" it was thereafter known. It is a pity to spoil so good a story, but the fact is that the word is derived from the French "sur" (upon) and "longe" (loin), and the preferable orthography would therefore be "surloin." However spelled, and whatever its history, the sirloin is deservedly popular.

Between the short and sirloin is the portion usually called the tenderloin, the name of which indicates its prevailing characteristic, the tenderness which makes it a much-to-be-desired cut in spite of its lack of juiciness and flavor as compared with other cuts.

The rib is the cut between the loin and chuck, and contains the best roasts. The fat on the best grade of ribs should be about one-half inch deep.

Round steaks are rather popular, but as Americans have a preference for loin and rib cuts, a large share of the lower grades of "rounds" are used otherwise, being converted into Hamburger, used as sausage trimmings and disposed of in many other ways.

Chucks are used extensively as shoulder steak, boiling pieces, and make very good roasts. Pot roasts are cut from the lower side, and stews or soup meat from the neck. The better grade of chucks should have a complete covering of fat, thickest at the rib end of the cut.

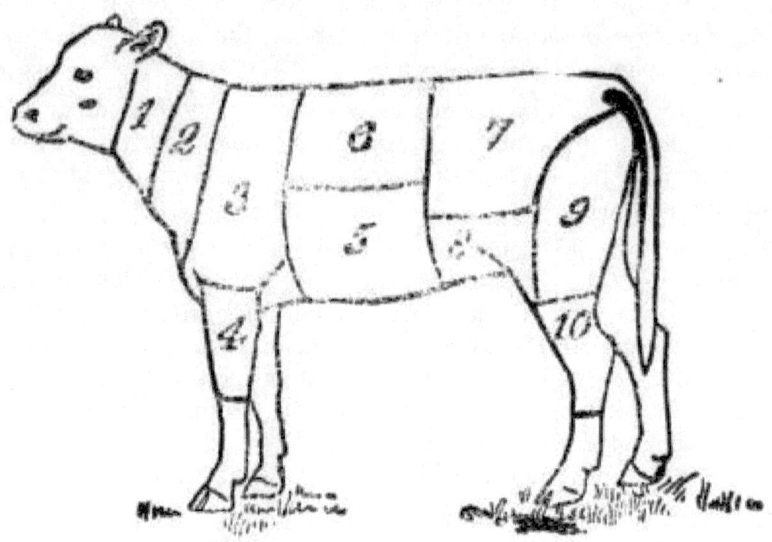

1. Neck. 2. Chuck. 3. Shoulder. 4. Fore shank. 5. Breast. 6. Ribs. 7. Loin. 8. Flank. 9. Leg. 10. Hind shank.

FIG. 2.—Diagrams of cuts of veal.

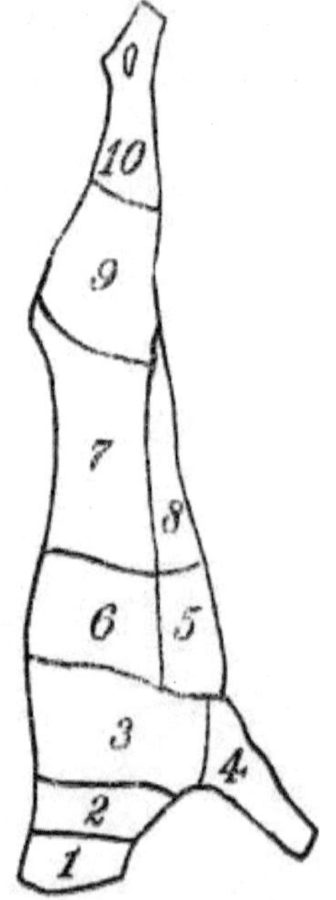

Quality in veal is determined by color and grain of flesh. It should be light pink, nearly white, and should contain a quantity of fat. The many ways of cooking and serving veal are so well known as to need but passing mention; veal loaf, veal cutlets, chops, pie, stew, curry of veal and many others are all favorite dishes in many homes.

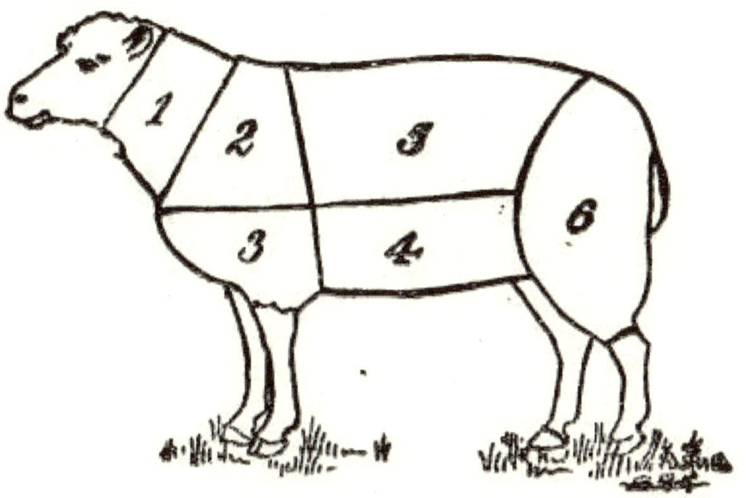

1. Neck. 2. Chuck. 3. Shoulder. 4. Flank.5. Loin. 6. Leg.

FIG. 3.—Diagrams of cuts of lamb and mutton.

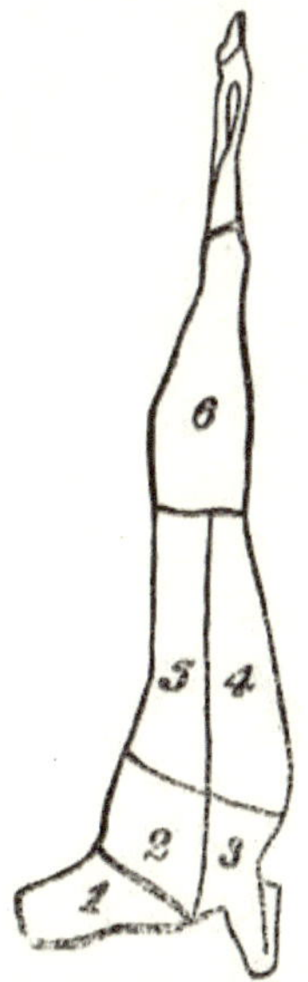

In selecting mutton or lamb we should be guided by color, fineness of grain, thickness of flesh and amount of fat. Mutton of a dull brick red is preferable, though the color varies from that to dark red. Lamb on account of its superior flavor is more popular than mutton. The flesh of lamb should be light in color, of fine grain and the fat evenly distributed. The nutritive value of mutton and lamb is practically the same as beef.

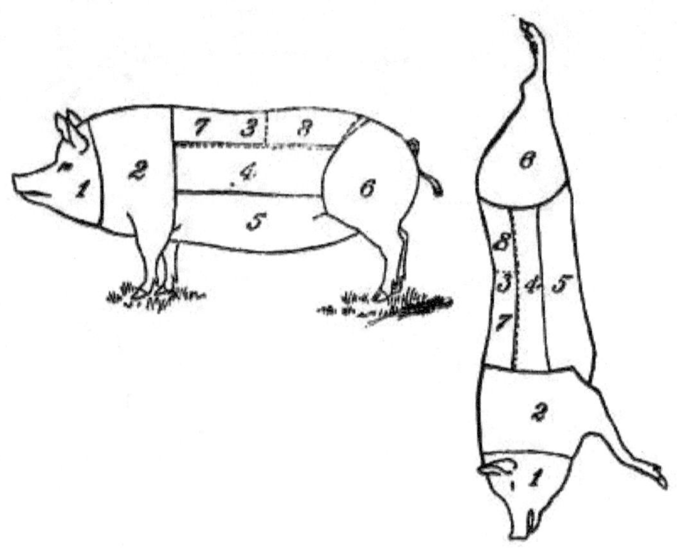

1. Head. 2. Shoulder. 3. Back. 4. Middle cut. 5. Belly. 6. Ham. 7. Ribs. 8. Loin.

FIG. 4.—Diagrams of cuts of pork.

The larger share of dressed pork is almost entirely clear fat, which should be white, firm and evenly distributed. Skin should be thin and smooth. Any detailed description of the various cuts of pork would be superfluous here. Not all our eloquence could adequately picture the delight with which an epicure gazes upon a ham boiled or baked by an experienced Kentucky or Virginia cook. The "roasting pig" is also a favorite in many places, and long has been, for, according to Irving, it was much prized by Ichabod Crane of Sleepy Hollow, and it has been mentioned by so great and learned a poet as Shakespeare.

Regarding all meats, we wish to say that as a rule the cheaper cuts have as much food value as the more expensive ones. Careful cooking will render the less expensive cuts delightfully appetizing. It is an advantage to housekeepers to know that meat need not be the highest in price to be nutritious and palatable.

BAKED BREAST OF MUTTON.

Sew up breast of mutton in a thin cloth, put into a stewpan, nearly cover with cold salt water, and let simmer, allowing ten minutes to each pound. Take out of pan and cloth, put into baking dish, rub over with mutton drippings, butter or fat, sprinkle with flour and bake one-half hour in hot oven, basting frequently with its own broth. Just before removing from oven, strew with bread crumbs and butter and let brown. Serve with brown sauce made from broth in which meat was cooked.

BEEF OMELET.

Three pounds chopped steak, three eggs, one and one-half cup rolled crackers, lump of butter size of a walnut, salt and pepper to taste, one-half cup milk. Mix thoroughly, make out in rolls, wrap in cloth, and bake two hours.

BEEFSTEAK WITH OYSTER BLANKET.

Broil an inch-thick sirloin steak, remove to platter, spread with butter, sprinkle with salt and pepper; cover steak with one pint of oysters, sprinkle with salt and pepper, dot with butter, place on grate in hot oven until the oysters are plump.

BEEF TENDERLOIN.

Take tenderloin of beef and lard it with pork. Put one can of mushrooms with the beef and cook in oven twenty minutes. Then cut the meat in slices one and one-half inch thick. On top of each slice place a few of the mushrooms and a little of the gravy, and set back in the oven five minutes to keep hot. Serve the slices on a chop plate, forming a circle, and filling in the center with peas.

BLANKETED HAM WITH SWEET POTATOES AND APPLES.

Cut off the fat close to the edge of a slice of ham one-half inch thick. Put fat through meat chopper, spread on top of ham, then sprinkle one-half cup of brown sugar and wine-glass of sherry over it. Peel and quarter four large sweet potatoes and four large apples. Put ham in oven in covered roasting pan. After it has cooked a quarter of an hour add apples and sweet potatoes. Now cook all of it three-quarters of an hour. This makes a delicious and savory dish, and is so substantial that little else is required for a meal.

BROWN STEW.

Thirty-five-cent beef off the shoulder; cut in pieces, cover with water and stew two hours until tender. Add one tablespoonful butter, and thicken with flour. Cook until brown.

CHICKEN CROQUETTE.

One-half pound chicken or veal, chopped very fine; season with one-half teaspoonful salt, one-half teaspoonful celery salt, one-fourth teaspoonful onion juice, one teaspoonful chopped parsley, one teaspoonful lemon juice, one saltspoonful white pepper, one-fourth saltspoonful cayenne. Mix with enough cream sauce to be easily handled; let cool, then shape into rolls. Roll on fine bread crumbs, dip in beaten egg, then roll in bread crumbs and fry in smoking-hot fat, drain on tissue paper. Boil meat in three quarts hot water, cold for soup, season with one teaspoonful salt, four grains pepper.

CHICKEN CROQUETTES.

Two pair sweetbreads, boiled and chopped fine, one teacupful boiled chicken chopped (use nothing but the white meat), one teacupful boiled bread and milk, pretty stiff; one-half pound butter, salt and pepper to taste, mold in shape, roll in cracker crumbs, beaten egg, and again in cracker crumbs, and fry in boiling lard.

Chicken Croquette Remarks.

Prepare meat and seasoning first. Put flour in hot butter dry, two tablespoonfuls cold water in the egg. Boil meat very slowly, until very tender. Make a hole in the flour when pouring in any liquid. Drop bread into hot fat, count forty slowly, until brown, fat then at proper heat. Cut a large potato in the hot grease; it takes out impurities.

CROQUETTES.

Cold turkey, chicken, veal or lamb, chopped fine; add one-fourth as much bread crumbs as meat; salt, pepper and herbs to taste; then to one cup of the mixture one well-beaten egg. Make in small balls egg-shaped, and fry in boiling lard.

FRICATELLI.

Chop raw fresh pork very fine, add salt and pepper and two small onions chopped fine, half as much stale bread as there is meat, soaked until soft, two eggs; mix all well together, make into oblong patties, and fry as you would oysters or other patties. A nice breakfast dish. Serve with sliced lemon.

HAM TOAST.

One-fourth pound of either boiled or fried ham; chop it fine, mix with the yolks of two eggs well beaten; one tablespoonful butter, enough cream or milk to make it soft, a little pepper; stir this over the fire until it thickens, dip toast into hot salted water for just an instant, spread with melted butter, then turn over the ham mixture. Dried beef may be substituted, adding, if fancied, a little chopped onion or parsley.

HUNGARIAN GOULASH.

Slice a peeled onion and cook it until brown in three tablespoonfuls of fat tried out of salt pork; take out the onion and turn in one and one-half pound lean uncooked veal cut into inch cubes. Stir and cook the meat until slightly browned, then, rejecting the fat, if there be any in the pan, place the meat in a casserole; add about a pint of broth or boiling water, a teaspoonful pepper, cover the dish and set to cook in the oven. In the meantime add more fat to the pan; when hot, brown in it a dozen balls cut from pared potatoes and a dozen small onions; when the onions are well browned, add to the casserole, and after the meat has been cooking an hour, add a teaspoonful salt and the potatoes, and if desired two tablespoonfuls flour mixed to a thin paste with cold water. Let cook in all about two hours. Serve from the casserole.

JELLIED VEAL.

A knuckle of veal, with the bone chopped; cover it with cold water and boil till the meat drops from the bone, pass the meat through a chopper; let the liquor continue boiling, as there must not be too much when you return it to the meat to cook a few minutes longer, adding pepper and salt to taste. Before removing from the fire, add quickly one egg. It is nice poured into individual molds.

LAMB AND RICE.

Cut lean lamb from the neck into small pieces. Put on in cold water and bring to a boil. Simmer for one and a half or two hours. Put in salt as desired soon after putting on to cook. When done add freshly boiled rice and simmer till the rice has absorbed the seasoning from the meat.

LIVER AND BACON.

Fry bacon till crisp. Then dip liver in the flour and fry until brown on both sides. Remove from skillet and cook in the skillet for a few minutes a chopped onion and a bunch of parsley. Then put back the liver and bacon, cover all with water and let simmer about one hour.

MEAT SOUFFLE.

Make one cup of cream sauce and season with chopped parsley and onion juice. Stir one cup chopped meat (chicken, fresh tongue, veal or lamb) into the sauce. When hot, add the beaten yolks of two eggs, cook one minute, and then set away to cool. When cool, stir in the whites, beaten stiff. Bake in a buttered dish about twenty minutes and serve immediately. If for lunch, serve with a mushroom sauce.

MEAT STEW.

Get five pounds of a cheap cut of beef. Cut into little pieces, taking off the fat. Try out the fat, brown the meat in it, and when well browned, cover with boiling water, boil five minutes, then cook in lower temperature until the meat is done. During the last hour of cooking add two-thirds cup of turnips and the same amount of carrots cut in small cubes, one-half an onion chopped fine, salt and pepper. About fifteen minutes before taking up put in four cups of potatoes cut in small pieces. Use one-quarter cup of flour for thickening and put in dumplings made as follows:

Mix and sift two cups flour, four teaspoonfuls baking powder, one-half teaspoonful salt. Work in two teaspoonfuls butter, add gradually two-thirds cup milk. Roll to one-half inch thick, and cut out with biscuit cutter.

POT ROAST.

Thirty-five-cent beef off the shoulder. Sear all over in hot fat, cover with water, add two cloves, one onion, one bay leaf, cover and cook slowly two and one-half hours. For gravy, thicken the liquor with flour.

POT ROAST. (OLD STYLE.)

Take a piece of fresh beef, about five or six pounds, not too fat. Put into a pot with just enough water to cover it. Set over a *slow* fire and let stew an hour, then add salt and pepper. Stew until tender, putting in a little onion if liked. Let nearly all the water boil away. When thoroughly tender take the meat out and pour the gravy in a bowl. Put a large lump of butter in the pot, dredge the meat with flour and return it to the pot to brown, turning it often to prevent burning. Skim fat from gravy poured off of meat; pour gravy in with the meat and stir in a large spoonful of flour; wet with a little water; let boil ten or fifteen minutes and pour into gravy dish. Try sometimes cooking in this way a piece of beef which has been placed in spiced pickle for two or three days.

RAGOUT OF BEEF.

Cut two pounds of the upper round of beef into inch squares, dredge them with salt and pepper and roll them in flour. Put into a saucepan some butter and some drippings, or a little suet, and let it fry out, using enough only to cover the bottom of the saucepan; when the grease is hot, turn in the pieces of meat and let them cook until well browned on all sides; watch and turn them as soon as browned, then draw the meat to one side of the pan and add a tablespoonful of flour; let the flour brown, and add a cupful of stock or water, and stir it until it comes to a boiling point; then add a teaspoonful of salt, one-half teaspoonful pepper, one-half teaspoonful kitchen bouquet, one carrot cut into blocks, and one teaspoonful onion; cover the saucepan, and let it simmer, not boil, for an hour. Serve a border of rice around the ragout.

ROAST BEEF.

Clean roast by wiping with a wet cloth. Place on a rack in oven, add suet to baste with. Cook a six-pound round roast an hour and twenty minutes; a three-rib roast one and one-half hour. Use no water.

ROUND STEAK.

Cover round steak with raw, chopped onions and bacon. Roll and tie. Put into deep kettle, sear or brown. Cover with water and pot roast for two hours. Boil down and thicken the gravy.

SMOTHERED OR POT-ROASTED BEEF.

Take four or five pounds of the middle of the rump, the flank or the round. Wipe with a clean, wet cloth and sear all over by placing in a hot frying pan and turning until all the surface is browned. Put it in a kettle with one-half pint of water, and place it where it will keep just below boiling point. Add just enough water now and then to keep meat from burning. Have close-fitting cover to keep in the steam. Cook until very tender. Serve hot or cold.

SPANISH STEAK.

Get round steak one and one-fourth inch thick. Cook the same as veal cutlets, only instead of using soup stock use one cup strained tomato juice and a little onion; a few mushrooms add to the flavor.

TURKEY DRESSING.

Cut crust off a loaf of bread, cut loaf in small bits, season with salt, pepper, sage, tablespoonful melted butter; beat one egg, add cup of milk and wet dressing.

VEAL BIRD.

Make a dressing of bread crumbs, melted butter, salt, pepper, and, if desired, a little sage. Cut veal cutlets into pieces about the size of palm of hand. Put a spoonful of dressing into each piece, roll, and fasten with a toothpick. Put in a pan with a cup of hot water or stock, cover and bake. Arrange around a platter or chop plate. Fill center with a pound of peas. This is delicious cooked in a fireless cooker.

VEAL CUTLETS.

Get a thick cutlet, one and a half inch thick, second cut with little round bone; have it scored on both sides. Then chop it all over on both sides with the edge of a china plate, until the meat is very ragged. Salt and pepper it, and rub flour into both sides until it will hold no more. Put two heaping tablespoonfuls of butter in a skillet and when hot put in the cutlet. Brown on both sides a golden brown, then add one cup of soup stock, or one cup boiling water, pouring it into the skillet. Let simmer one hour.

VEAL LOAF.

Three pounds of raw veal chopped very fine, butter size of an egg, three eggs, three tablespoonfuls cream or milk. Mix the eggs and cream together. Mix with the veal four pounded crackers, one teaspoonful black pepper, one large tablespoonful salt, one large teaspoonful sage. Mix well together and form into a loaf. Bake two and one-half hours, basting with butter and water while baking. Serve cut in thin slices.

VEAL LOAF.

Three pounds of veal chopped fine, one-half pound salt or fresh pork, one cup powdered crackers, one cup water, two eggs, three teaspoonfuls salt, three teaspoonfuls sage, one teaspoonful pepper. Bake in rather quick oven.

VEAL PIE.

Crust for veal or chicken pie, two teacups flour, two teaspoonfuls baking powder, one teaspoonful salt, two tablespoonfuls shortening; beat one egg and fill the teacup with milk, add to flour. Boil veal in cold water until quite tender, keep out a quart of the broth after it is cooked. When two-thirds done put in the salt.

GRAVY FOR PIE.

Two tablespoonfuls melted butter, three tablespoonfuls flour; mix well, add salt and pepper, one cup cream, slightly warm; stir in the quart of broth after thickening is added. Cook about fifteen minutes, stir, but do not boil. Put meat and gravy in baking dish, cover with dough and bake twenty minutes.

EGGS

Eggs should be kept in cool places. If a recipe calls for just the white of an egg, the yolk may be kept from hardening by putting in a cup of cold water. Eggs may be cooked soft in two ways: Pour boiling water over the egg and cover them from five to ten minutes. Second method: Put eggs into cold water, and when water bubbles they are cooked.

BAKED EGGS.

Twelve hard-boiled eggs, one-half pint cream, butter size of an egg, one teaspoonful fine chopped parsley, one tablespoonful flour, salt and pepper. Mix cream, butter, flour and parsley. Cook till thick. Slice eggs, after each layer of eggs one of bread crumbs; cover with sauce, then bread crumbs, and bake till brown.

CHEESE OMELET.

Four eggs, four tablespoonfuls cold water, one-fourth teaspoonful salt, three level tablespoonfuls grated cheese, two level tablespoonfuls melted butter. Put butter in saucepan, separate whites from yolks. For omelet do not beat yolks too long, only until lemon color. To yolks add water and salt. Beat whites and pour yolks over whites; fold and cut with a spoon. *Do not beat.* Pour in saucepan, loosen with a knife around edges, cook until it sets. Sprinkle grated cheese on top and put in oven for two or three minutes. Serve very hot. Old English dairy cheese is the best.

EGG CUTLETS.

Heaping tablespoonful of butter. When hot, stir in two heaping tablespoonfuls flour, one-half pint of milk, and stir until smooth and well cooked; chop three hard-boiled eggs, and stir in after taking from the fire. Season with salt, pepper and one-half teaspoonful of onion juice; also add parsley. Put away until cold, mold and roll in cracker crumbs, and fry in abundance of hot fat. This may be used for meat croquettes, substituting chopped meat, cooked, for eggs.

EGGS SHIRRED IN TOMATOES.

Cut circular pieces out from the stem end of round tomato and remove part of the pulp. Season with salt and pepper; also with onion, juice and parsley, if liked. Break an egg into each tomato and put in a slow oven until each egg is set. Serve on hot buttered toast.

POACHED EGGS.

Partly fill a shallow pan with boiling water. Break eggs singly into a saucer, sliding each as broken into the boiling water. Keep pan where water will not quite boil. With a spoon baste the water over the yolk until it is covered thinly with white. Remove each egg with a skimmer, trim off ragged edges, and serve on buttered toast.

SHIRRED EGGS.

Shirred eggs are a pleasant change from the usual boiled eggs for breakfast. Drop each egg carefully into a buttered ramikin, season with pepper, salt and a small lump of butter. Set ramikin in a shallow pan filled with water, place in moderate oven and cook until whites are firm.

SOFT BOILED, OR STEAMED EGGS.

Put the desired number of eggs into a kettle and cover with boiling water. Cover the kettle and let stand ten minutes. Drain off the water, put eggs into a bowl, cover again with boiling water and send to the table.

VEGETABLES

"Perhaps if we could penetrate Nature's secrets we should find that what we call weeds are more essential to the well-being of the world than the most precious fruit or grain." — Hawthorne.

The simplest methods of cooking and serving vegetables are generally the best. The most common method of cooking them is in boiling water. All green vegetables, bulbs and tubers should be crisp and firm when put on to cook, and should, of course, be thoroughly cleaned before being cooked.

Almost all vegetables may be served in the form of salad. Our most common green salad plant is lettuce; celery is next, but endive, chicory and dandelion, with many others, may be used to advantage in this way, and furnish pleasing variety to the menu.

Nearly all vegetables are good canned, and if care is taken in preparing and canning, it is possible to have fresh-tasting fruits and vegetables through all seasons.

Thorough sterilization is necessary in canning or preserving. In the first place, use good jars. Glass jars will be found the most satisfactory. Those with glass top and rubber ring held in place by a wire spring are the cheapest in the long run, although the initial expense may be somewhat high. Never use defective rubbers, as vegetables often spoil after being sterilized, because of bad rubbers.

A clothes boiler makes a good container to use in sterilizing. A false bottom made of wire netting cut to fit or strips of wood may be used, as the jars will break if set flat on the bottom of the boiler.

Select vegetables that have not begun to harden or decay. Always can as soon as possible after gathering. Some vegetables are best cooked before putting in jars; among these are beets, pumpkins and turnips, but most of them may be packed while raw in jars and cooked as follows:

Pack jar full, adding salt as desired, fill with cold water to the top of the jar. Put the rubber on the jar and place the glass top on, but do not press down the spring at the side of the jar. Put as many jars in the boiler as it will hold without crowding. Pour into the boiler enough water (cold) to prevent it from going dry during the boiling. Put the cover on the boiler and bring the water to a boil and keep it boiling for an hour. (Hour and a half for half-gallon jars.) At the end of this time remove the boiler cover, and let the steam escape. Press down the spring on each jar, which clamps on the top, and no outside air can enter.

On the next day raise the spring at the side of the jar and boil as on the first day, clamping on the top as before at the end of operation. Repeat this on the third day. All meats, fruits and vegetables are sterilized on this principle.

Never subject jars to a draft of cold air when removing them from the boiler, as this will be likely to crack them. If, after sterilization seems complete, any jars spoil, increase the time of boiling.

ASPARAGUS.

Cut the tender part into short pieces. Cover with boiling water, and boil until done. Season with salt and pepper, and serve with most of juice; or, if preferred, serve with a cream dressing.

BEETS.

Wash the beets carefully without breaking the skin. Cover with boiling water and boil until tender. Take from the boiling water and drop into cold. Rub off the skin, cut in thin slices and serve at once with salt and butter.

CINCINNATI BAKED BEANS.

Measure beans (marrowfat are best), put them in cold water and parboil fifteen minutes and drain; use the Boston bean pot. For three pints of dried beans add three level teaspoonfuls salt, one-quarter pound pickled pork cut fine, six tablespoonfuls New Orleans molasses or six tablespoonfuls of C sugar, one tablespoonful standard mustard. Mix the above well and put in a three-quart bean pot, and fill within one inch of top with boiling water. May be kept in oven several days, but must never be allowed to get dry, adding boiling water as needed.

CORN.

Cook ears of corn five minutes in boiling water. Then cut through the center of each row of grains and press the grains from the hulls with the back of a knife. Put corn in saucepan and season with butter, salt, pepper and sugar. Add enough hot milk to moisten, and cook ten minutes.

When succotash is desired, add to a pint of corn cooked as above the same amount of cooked and seasoned shelled beans.

CORN PUDDING.

One dozen ears of corn, two eggs, one kitchen spoonful butter, one-half teaspoonful salt, one tablespoonful sugar.

CORN PUDDING.

To one can of corn, one pint milk, three eggs, two tablespoonful melted butter, one tablespoonful white sugar, pepper and salt to taste. Beat the eggs very light, add sugar and butter rubbed together; stir hard. Next the corn and seasoning, finally the milk; beat hard, bake in buttered dish one-half hour, covered; then lift top and brown. Serve in baking dish.

CREAMED CAULIFLOWER.

One pint cooked cauliflower, one pint milk, one teaspoonful salt, one-third teaspoonful pepper, one tablespoonful butter, one-half teaspoonful flour, three slices toasted bread. Break cooked cauliflower into branches and season with half of the salt and pepper. Put butter in a saucepan on the fire. When hot add flour and stir until frothy and smooth. Add gradually the milk, constantly stirring. When sauce boils add the salt, pepper and cauliflower. Cook ten minutes and serve very hot on the slices of toast.

GREEN STUFFED PEPPERS.

Clean out peppers and stuff with rice or potatoes, and meat. Moisten with hot water, standing on end in baking dish. Cover and bake until almost done, then remove cover and brown. Cheese or tomatoes may be used instead of meat.

HASHED BROWN POTATOES.

Boil about one quart potatoes, drain and sprinkle with one teaspoonful salt and a little pepper. Add one teaspoonful chopped parsley and a few drops of onion juice, brown one heaping tablespoonful butter, add one tablespoonful flour and gradually one cup hot water. Salt and pepper to taste. Add potatoes, and cook about five minutes, or until they have absorbed nearly all the sauce. Butter a saute pan, add the potatoes and cook until light brown. Turn over like an omelet. Potatoes must not be chopped until cold.

HASHED TURNIPS.

Chop boiled turnips into large pieces. Put in saucepan, and for a pint and a half of turnips add a teaspoonful of pepper, a tablespoonful of butter and four tablespoonfuls of water. Cook over a hot fire until seasoning is absorbed.

HOME-MADE NOODLES.

(Serve as a Vegetable with Stewed Chicken or Veal.)

Four eggs, one tablespoonful cream, one teaspoonful salt, flour enough to make a stiff dough; roll out very thin and let dry an hour or longer; roll up and cut into fine strips; put into a kettle of boiling water, salted, boil ten minutes; cut a few noodles an inch wide and fry brown in butter to place on top. Serve with plenty of gravy.

KALE CANNON.

(OLD IRISH DISH.)

Take ten or twelve good-sized potatoes, peel and boil in salt water, add a large bunch of parsley previously washed and drained, and a pinch of baking soda. When the parsley is done, which will be in ten or fifteen minutes, take it up and lay it in a plate, drain it well and chop it, leaving out the stems. Chop fine one onion; when the potatoes are cooked place them at the back of the stove with a cloth and the lid over them; mash them, adding the onions as quickly as possible as the hot potatoes cook it, add a little pepper and salt and about one-half cup of hot milk with a lump of butter melted in it. Mix all together, serve with a little butter with each helping. This is sometimes made with kale, hence its name.

LYONNAISE POTATOES.

One pint cold potatoes cut in dice and seasoned with salt and pepper. Fry one scant tablespoonful of onion in one heaping tablespoonful of butter, add the potatoes, stir with a fork until the potatoes absorb the butter, add one teaspoonful chopped parsley. Three pints of boiling water, one-half teaspoonful salt. All vegetables should be put in boiling water.

MOCK ASPARAGUS.

Cut the tops from several bunches of young, green onions, leaving the stalks about the length of asparagus; trim the roots, wash and tie in bundles like asparagus. Cook until tender, drain off water, sprinkle with cheese and pour over ends a little melted butter. Onions are very delicate prepared in this way.

MUSHROOM SPAGHETTI.

Boil spaghetti in salt water one-half hour, drain, cover with soup stock, add one can of tomatoes, salt, pepper to taste. One can mushrooms. Boil all these ingredients well together, turn into a hot dish. Pass grated Parmesan cheese, to sprinkle over each portion. Fresh mushrooms turned in butter may be used instead of canned ones.

NEW ENGLAND SWEET POTATOES.

Put a layer of boiled, peeled and sliced sweet potatoes in a greased baking dish, sprinkle with brown sugar and dot with butter. Cover with another layer of potatoes and another of sugar, and so on until the dish is full. The last thing, pour over a cup of boiling water. Bake in a medium oven for one-half hour.

OKRA.

This vegetable grows in almost every state in the Union and is used extensively in soups. When young it is good boiled in salted water until tender, drained, and heated for five minutes with cream, butter, salt and pepper.

BAKED ONIONS.

Cover a number of large onions with boiling water and boil twenty minutes. Drain off water and make small hole in center of each onion. Fill hole with well-seasoned mashed potatoes. Add salt, pepper and butter, and milk to cover. Bake about one-half hour.

PARSNIPS.

Wash and scrape until clean, and cook until tender. When cooked, put into hot dish, sprinkle with salt and add bits of butter. Serve at once.

PEAS AND CARROTS.

One cup of carrots cut in dice and cooked, two cups green peas (or canned), four tablespoonfuls cream, one tablespoonful butter, salt and pepper. Put carrots and peas in stew pan, add cream, butter, and serve hot.

POTATOES AU GRATIN.

First prepare your white sauce of one-half pint milk, one tablespoonful butter, two tablespoonfuls flour. Cream butter and flour and add to boiling milk. Cook about ten minutes in double boiler. Slice or chop cold boiled potatoes, put in baking dish. One layer of potatoes. Cover thickly with layer of white sauce and grated cheese. Season with salt, pepper, mustard and cayenne pepper to suit taste. Put in other layers in same manner and bake twenty minutes.

POTATO CROQUETTES.

Two cups hot riced potatoes, one-half teaspoonful salt, one-fourth teaspoonful celery salt, one teaspoonful finely chopped parsley, two tablespoonfuls butter, one-half teaspoonful pepper, yolk of one egg, a few drops of onion juice. Mix the above ingredients, beat until light, shape, egg and crumb, and fry in deep fat, drain on paper. Serve hot. Finely chopped almonds are a pleasant addition.

POTATOES O'BRIEN.

Boil with skin on, allow them to stand until perfectly cold. Peel and chop fine and use Spanish peppers and salt, cream and butter. If you wish to brown, don't use cream, just fry slowly in butter.

POTATOES ON HALF SHELL.

Six baked potatoes, three tablespoonfuls hot milk, two tablespoonfuls butter, whites of two eggs, salt and pepper. Cut slice from top, scoop out inside, mash, add seasoning, then the whites of the eggs well beaten. Refill and bake from five to eight minutes in hot oven. A little grated cheese can be sprinkled on them.

RICH CREAMED POTATOES.

One cup potatoes cold, milk to cover, three tablespoonfuls butter, salt and pepper to taste, dash of paprika. Cut cold boiled potatoes in dice, better if boiled the day before. Melt butter in a saucepan, add potatoes and seasoning, cover and cook a minute, uncover, stir well, cover and cook another minute. Then add milk to cover well, and cook very slowly for forty-five minutes, keeping saucepan covered. These need watching, but are delicious; nice for Sunday night supper. Asbestos mats are best to use under these, if cooked over gas stove.

SALSIFY.

To prevent salsify from turning dark, drop as soon as pared into a mixture of flour, water and a little vinegar. After paring, cut into slices about three inches long. Put on in prepared water and cook thirty minutes from the time it begins to boil. Drain and serve in white sauce; or mix butter, salt, lemon juice and parsley and serve with this.

SCALLOPED CELERY.

Chopped celery, bread or cracker crumbs, butter, salt and pepper, milk. Place a layer of crumbs in bottom of buttered dish, then a layer of celery, dot with butter, season and continue alternately until pan is full, having crumbs on top, cover with milk, bake slowly until milk is absorbed, about one-half hour. Serve in bake dish.

SCALLOPED POTATOES AND EGGS.

Boil six medium-sized potatoes in salt water; boil four eggs an hour; let get cold. Make a cream sauce of one heaping tablespoonful of butter and a rounding tablespoonful of flour, with one and one-half cup of milk and a little salt. Cut potatoes and eggs and put in baking dish with the white sauce. Sprinkle buttered bread crumbs over the top. Bake until a yellowish brown, about three-fourths of an hour.

SHELLED BEANS STEWED.

Cut one-quarter pound salt pork in slices and fry slowly for ten minutes. Add one onion, chopped fine, and cook very slowly for twenty minutes. Cover one quart of green shelled kidney beans with boiling water and boil ten minutes. Drain off the water, put the beans and one tablespoonful of flour with the pork and onion and stir over the fire for five minutes. Add a quart of boiling water and one-half teaspoonful pepper. Keep where it will simmer for two hours. Salt to taste.

SPAGHETTI.

Four onions cut fine, one can of tomatoes, one package spaghetti, grated cheese, salt, pepper and cinnamon. Fry four onions in butter and lard, then put in tomatoes and seasoning, boil slowly until thick, put in grated cheese. Boil spaghetti in hot water until tender, cook until done, throw into strainer, then serve. Place grated cheese over it. Serve sauce separately.

SPAGHETTI.

White sauce: One and one-half cup hot milk, tablespoonful butter, tablespoonful flour. Add one-half teaspoonful salt and mix two-thirds cup fine cracker crumbs with one-third cup melted butter and sprinkle over the top. One-half cup cheese, dry.

SPINACH.

Put one-half peck spinach in stewpan and on the fire. Cover and cook for ten minutes. Press down and turn over several times. At the end of ten minutes turn into chopping bowl and mince. Return to stewpan and add seasoning; two generous tablespoonfuls butter and teaspoonful salt. Simmer for ten minutes.

SPINACH WITH SAUCE.

One-half peck spinach, one teaspoonful salt, two tablespoonfuls flour or corn-starch, one pint boiling water, two tablespoonfuls butter, three-fourths cup cream or one cup milk. Prepare one-half peck spinach by cooking uncovered in one pint of boiling water, or, if young and tender, its own juices. Drain and chop fine. Put two tablespoonfuls butter in a frying pan; when melted add the spinach and cook three minutes. Sprinkle with two level tablespoonfuls cornstarch; stir thoroughly and add gradually three-fourths cup milk. Cook five minutes, serve with toast points on a pretty platter.

SQUASH.

Cut squash into small pieces and either steam or cook in boiling water. If boiled it will cook in half an hour; steaming will take an hour. Mash fine, season with salt, pepper and butter.

TOMATO ON TOAST.

Boil a quart of peeled and cut tomatoes for about ten minutes, then strain and put in saucepan with two teaspoonfuls salt, one-half teaspoonful pepper and two tablespoonfuls butter. Cook for five minutes. Cover a hot platter with toasted slices of bread and pour the tomato over it.

TWENTY-MINUTE CABBAGE.

Cut cabbage fine as for slaw. Cover with *boiling* water and boil twenty minutes, changing the water once. Drain and serve with sauce made of tablespoonful butter, tablespoonful flour, cup of hot milk.

DESSERTS

"The little sweet doth kill much bitterness." —Keats.

ALMOND TART.

Yolks of six eggs, beaten well, to which is added one cup powdered sugar. Mix one cup grated dried rusk, one cup grated almonds, one teaspoonful baking powder. Add to the yolks, and lastly add the well-beaten whites of six eggs. This makes three layers. Bake very slowly.

FILLING.

One cup hot water, to which is added one-half cup sugar, one egg, one tablespoonful cornstarch, boil slowly, and add one cup grated almonds and one teaspoonful vanilla. Any other nuts can be used.

APPLE CHARLOTTE.

One cup apple sauce, one cup sugar, one-third package gelatin, three cups cold water, three cups boiling water, one lemon. Dissolve the gelatin (Knox's preferred) in cold water for five minutes, add the boiling water, sugar, lemon juice and apple, strain and set it to cool. When it is nearly stiff, add the well-beaten whites of three eggs. Line a mold with lady-fingers, pour in jelly and let stand until firm. It is nice served with whipped cream or a sauce made from yolks of eggs.

SAUCE.

One pint boiling milk, yolks of three eggs, one-fourth cup sugar. Add a tablespoonful gelatin dissolved in a little water just before taking from fire. A teaspoonful of vanilla.

APRICOT SHORTCAKE.

Three cups flour, two teaspoonfuls baking powder, one-half teaspoonful salt, one-half cup butter, one egg (very light), one cup cold water stirred into the flour. Stir all very slowly. Divide in half, bake in square pans. Sprinkle the tops with white granulated sugar. Bake ten or fifteen minutes. Mash and sweeten the fruit, spread on top and between layers.

SAUCE.

One teaspoonful cornstarch with one-half cup sugar; one cup of the fruit juice at boiling point, add sugar with cornstarch and let boil five minutes. Grease pans with lard or beef drippings.

BAKED APPLES.

Core the apples, but do not peel them. Stuff them with minced pecans mixed with scraped maple sugar, and bake. When done, cover with whipped cream.

BAKED APPLES.

Pare and quarter apples. Put into baking dish with butter, sugar, cinnamon and a little hot water. Keep cover on dish until almost done, then remove cover and brown.

BAKED DUMPLINGS.

For the dough: One pint flour, one-half cup butter, stir together; one teaspoonful baking powder, and milk to make a dough. Roll, cut in squares. Fill with apple or any fruit desired, put dumplings in a pan with one pint of water, a little butter, two-thirds cup sugar. Put on top of stove and let come to a boil, then put in oven at least one-half hour. Serve warm with cream.

BREAD PUDDING.

One pint bread crumbs without crust to one quart milk, four eggs beaten separately. After it is baked, cover with sweet jelly, beat the whites very light, add to them one-half cup pulverized sugar, put on top of the pudding, then in the oven until brown.

SAUCE.

Two tablespoonfuls butter, one-half cup sugar, yolk of one egg, one tablespoonful cornstarch; beat hard, thin with boiling water, cook in hot water.

CABINET PUDDING.

Butter a melon mold, decorated with seeded raisins; one layer lady-fingers or stale sponge cake, then a few raisins, then repeat until the mold is nearly full; beat well the yolks of three eggs, add three tablespoonfuls sugar, one-half saltspoonful salt, add slowly one pint boiling milk, pour over cake in mold, and then steam for one hour. Serve with Foamy Sauce.

Foamy Sauce.

Rub one-half cup butter to a cream, add slowly one cup powdered sugar, one teaspoonful vanilla. When ready to serve, add one-fourth cup boiling water, the whites of two eggs beaten to a foam.

CHOCOLATE PUDDING.

One pint milk, four tablespoonfuls sugar, one teaspoonful vanilla, salt, two tablespoonfuls cornstarch, one tablespoonful cocoa, cinnamon. Thoroughly blend together the dry cornstarch and cocoa, then dissolve with a little cold milk and reduce to a pouring state, add vanilla. Heat the milk in a double boiler, add sugar and a pinch of cinnamon and salt; when scalding hot, pour in cornstarch and cocoa mixture and stir carefully until it thickens well. Turn into wet molds. Serve with plain or whipped cream. Garnish with Maraschino cherry.

CHOCOLATE PUDDING.

One pint milk, one pint bread crumbs, yolks of three eggs, one-half teaspoon vanilla, five tablespoonfuls grated chocolate. Scald the milk, add bread crumbs and chocolate. Take from fire and add one-half cup sugar and the beaten yolks. Bake in pudding dish fifteen minutes. Make meringue of whites of eggs and three tablespoonfuls of powdered sugar. Spread over pudding and brown. Serve warm or cold, with cream, plain or whipped.

CREAM STRAWBERRY SHORTCAKE.

One quart white flour; mix well with three tablespoonfuls cold butter, one teaspoonful salt, a tablespoonful white sugar. Add a beaten egg to a cup of sour cream, turn into other ingredients. Dissolve a teaspoonful of soda in a little water, mix all together quickly, roll lightly into two round sheets, place on pie tins and bake from twenty to twenty-five minutes in quick oven. Split, spread sweetened berries between layers and on top, and cover generously with whipped cream.

CUP CUSTARD.

Beat four eggs and stir in one-half cup sugar, one-fourth teaspoonful salt, then slowly one quart scalded milk. When sugar has dissolved, flavor with nutmeg or vanilla and pour in cups or bake dish. Set cups or bake dish in a pan of hot water and bake in a moderate oven till a knife inserted in custard comes out clean. Do not let the water in the pan boil. Serve plain or with caramel sauce.

CARAMEL SAUCE.

Melt one-half cup sugar to a syrup of light brown color, and add one-half cup water. Simmer ten minutes. Cool before serving.

FIG PUDDING.

Chop one-half pound beef suet and work with the hands until creamy, then add one-half pound figs finely chopped, and again work with the hands until thoroughly blended. Soak two cups stale bread crumbs in one-half cup milk thirty minutes. Add two eggs well beaten, one cup sugar and three-fourths teaspoonful salt. Combine the mixture, beat vigorously, turn into a buttered mold, steam over three hours, remove from the mold and serve with sauce. Serve ten or eleven persons.

SAUCE FOR PUDDING.

Yolks of two eggs beaten light, two-thirds cup powdered sugar, one teaspoonful vanilla. Add one-half pint cream, whipped just before serving. Whites of eggs may be used instead of whipped cream.

FIG TAPIOCA.

Soak two-thirds of a cup of tapioca in three cups of cold water, add one pound of chopped figs and one and one-half cup of brown sugar. Steam one hour. Just before the tapioca sets add one cupful of chopped nuts and one teaspoonful of vanilla, (with knife), one-fourth teaspoonful salt. Ice water to form stiff dough.

FLUFFY CORNSTARCH PUDDING.

One pint of milk, three tablespoonfuls sugar, two tablespoonfuls cornstarch, whites of three eggs, a little salt to taste, one-half teaspoonful vanilla or lemon. Have egg whites beaten stiff. Put milk on in a double boiler; when heated, add sugar, salt and flavoring; when scalding hot, add cornstarch, which has been dissolved in a little cold milk. Let this cook a minute or two, stirring well, then add the stiffly beaten whites of eggs, using cut-and-fold method. Turn mixture into molds which have been wet with cold water; sherbet cups make excellent molds, tea cup half filled will do. Turn into suitable dishes and serve with custard sauce. Maraschino cherry on top of pudding is attractive.

CUSTARD SAUCE.

One pint milk, yolks of three eggs, three tablespoonfuls sugar, one teaspoonful vanilla or lemon, little salt. Beat egg yolks, add to these the sugar; heat milk in a double boiler, add salt and beaten egg yolks, stirring until the mixture thickens. Flavor when cool.

FROZEN PUDDING.

Soak one cup of candied fruit cut in pieces; put in hot syrup (sugar and water) to cover until softened; mix one quart cream and three-fourths cup sugar, and flavor, then freeze. Line two-quart mold with lady-fingers, crust side down. Fill with alternate layers of cream and fruit, cover, pack in salt and ice and let stand two hours. Serve with a nice boiled custard or whipped cream.

FRUIT PUFFS.

Make dough as for dumplings or fruit roll, only stiff enough to drop from spoon. To one pint sifted flour add one heaping teaspoonful baking powder, one-fourth teaspoonful salt, lump of lard or butter size of small egg, milk to make dough of consistency to drop it from a tablespoon. Drop a little dough on top of fruit, having cup about two-thirds full. Place cups in steamer and steam about three-fourths of an hour. Serve with any sauce or dip preferred.

FRUIT ROLL.

One pint flour, one tablespoonful sugar, one teaspoonful baking powder, pinch of salt, rounding tablespoonful lard, milk enough to roll. Roll in a long piece and put fruit (ripe or canned peaches, apricots, raspberries, blackberries or cherries) in center, then put the two sides together, a little water will make it stick; turn over and put in pan. Butter the top, take one-half cup sugar and one tablespoonful flour, mix thoroughly and pour into this the juice of the fruit or a little boiling water. Put a little of this on the top, also a little nutmeg. When half baked, pour in the sugar and flour, water or juice of fruit. Bake about one-half hour, when done baste with the juice. Serve with cream and sugar.

GRAHAM PUDDING.

One and one-half cup of Graham flour, one cup sweet milk, one-half cup molasses, one cup chopped raisins, one-half teaspoonful salt, one level teaspoonful soda. Sift the Graham flour to make it light and return the bran to the sifted mixture; dissolve the soda in the milk and add the salt and molasses with the milk to the Graham flour. Then add the raisins and pour into a double boiler and steam four hours.

GREEN TOMATO PIE.

Pare and slice tomatoes just beginning to ripen. Fill heaping full pie pan prepared with lower crust. Put in one cup sugar, a little nutmeg or cinnamon, juice of half a lemon and a tablespoonful butter. Cover with top crust. Bake three-fourths hour.

ICE CREAM PUDDING.

Custard: Two tablespoonfuls cornstarch, yolks of three eggs, one cup milk, one and one-third cup pulverized sugar; boil in double boiler, stirring constantly. Whip one quart cream, sweeten and flavor to taste; dissolve one tablespoonful Cox's gelatine and mix with cream; then add the beaten whites of eggs to the cream. Place alternate layers of the custard and whipped cream in a form or mold, sprinkling blanched and chopped almonds and candied cherries cut in small pieces in each layer. Close mold securely and place in a pail of chopped ice and salt. Allow four hours for freezing. Turn out of mold on a platter and cut in slices.

LEMON BUTTER.

Two lemons, grate rind of one; two eggs, one cup of sugar and small piece of butter. Boil until it thickens.

LEMON JELLY.

Soak one-half box of gelatine in one-half cup cold water; dissolve with one cup boiling water. Juice of one lemon, one cup sugar, one pint orange juice. Strain through a fine napkin. Put on ice to harden.

LEMON SAUCE.

Two heaping teaspoonfuls cornstarch, one cup sugar, add two cups boiling water, let simmer ten minutes, add grated rind and juice of one lemon, one tablespoonful butter.

MACARONI SOUFFLE.

Melt three tablespoonfuls butter, add four tablespoonfuls flour, and gradually one cup scalded milk with one-half cup macaroni rolled fine; when well thickened, pour into yolks of four eggs, beaten until thick, and lemon color, and mix with two tablespoonfuls sugar; cool, add one-fourth teaspoonful Crown almond extract and cut and fold in the whites of four eggs, beaten till stiff and dry. Turn into buttered pudding dish, sprinkle with macaroni crumbs and bake from thirty to thirty-five minutes in slow oven in a pan of water. Serve with Foamy Sauce.

FOAMY SAUCE.

Beat whites of two eggs till stiff, add gradually one cup powdered sugar and continue beating, and then add one-fourth cup hot milk or cream and one teaspoonful vanilla.

MAPLE MOUSSE.

Three-fourths cup maple syrup, yolks of four eggs, one pint whipped cream. Beat yolks until light, cook in double boiler with syrup fifteen minutes. Stir rapidly. Beat until cold, add whipped cream, put in a mold and pack in ice four or five hours.

MARSHMALLOW PUDDING.

Dissolve one and one-half tablespoonful gelatine in one-half cup boiling water. When thoroughly dissolved, add one-half cup cold water into which has been stirred a pinch of salt and sugar to taste; set aside to cool. When the gelatine begins to thicken, pour it slowly into the stiffly beaten whites of four eggs, beating it well as you pour. The mixture will now be white and spongy. Pour into mold or dish one-half of mixture, flavored to taste. Have ready cocoanut, chopped nuts or Maraschino cherries (all three may be used) in a center layer. Onto this pour the remainder of the mixture, which may be colored if desired. With this serve a sauce made from the yolks of three eggs, one pint milk, sugar and vanilla to taste; cook in double boiler till it thickens so that it will pour nicely. Quick and easy to prepare.

MOCK CHARLOTTE RUSSE.

One round tablespoonful cornstarch, moisten in cold water. Pour over one-half pint of boiling water, boil one minute, add one-half cup sugar and pour while hot over the well-beaten whites of three eggs. Add a teaspoonful vanilla and turn into a mold to harden. Make a sauce from the three yolks of the eggs beaten with four tablespoonfuls sugar and one pint of scalded milk cooked together for a moment, but not allowed to boil, or it will curdle.

ORANGE ICE.

Boil one quart of water, add one pint of sugar, boil twenty minutes, cool, add one pint orange juice, grated rind of two oranges and one-fourth cup lemon juice. Freeze and serve.

ORANGE PUDDING.

Four large oranges, sliced thin and sprinkled with sugar. Make a boiled custard of one pint milk, yolks of three eggs, pinch of salt, one tablespoonful cornstarch, three tablespoonfuls sugar. When cold, pour over oranges, cover with beaten whites and one-half cup sugar. To be eaten cold. Whipped cream can be used instead of frosting.

PINEAPPLE SHERBET.

Soak one tablespoonful gelatine in a cup of cold water; when soft, dissolve with a cup of boiling water, strain, add one pint sugar and one-half pint grated pineapple, juice of one lemon. Put in a freezer, pack with ice and salt and freeze.

PLUM PUDDING.

One and one-half cup molasses, one and one-half cup suet cut fine, one and one-half cup milk, one pound raisins, one pound currants, three teaspoonfuls soda melted in a little water, then poured in the molasses and stirred; cinnamon and cloves to taste, flour enough to make a stiff batter.

SAUCE.

One large cup brown sugar, one-half cup butter beat until light, two eggs beaten separately; flavor with vanilla, put on stove and stir until it creams.

PLUM PUDDING.

Three cups flour, one cup bread crumbs, one and one-half cup sweet milk, three-fourths cup cider, one cup sugar, one-half pound raisins, one-half pound currants, one-half pound suet, one nutmeg, two ounces citron, one teaspoonful cinnamon, one teaspoonful baking powder, one-half teaspoonful mace, yolks of four eggs, whites of two eggs. Boil five hours.

PLUM PUDDING.

Five-cent bakers' loaf of bread, one and one-half cup stoned raisins, one cup currants, one-fourth cup citron, one cup suet, one cup New Orleans molasses, one saltspoonful cloves, one tablespoonful cinnamon, two eggs, two teaspoonfuls baking powder, one cup flour, heaping. Soak loaf of bread thoroughly in cold water, then squeeze dry. Steam five or six hours. Serves sixteen persons.

PRUNE PUDDING.

Cook twelve large prunes until soft. Strain through a colander. Beat the whites of four eggs stiff and add one cup cracker or dried rusk crumbs, one cup powdered sugar and pulp of prunes. Boil in double boiler about one and one-half hours and serve with whipped cream.

PRUNE WHIP.

One-half pound prunes, one-half cup sugar, one-fourth teaspoonful lemon juice, white of one egg. Beat white of egg to stiff froth, add slowly three teaspoon-fuls prunes, pressed through a sieve, then the lemon juice and sugar. The prunes should be soaked over night in enough water to cover; cook in same water till soft. Remove stones and force through a strainer (use the yolk of egg for custard sauce). One egg yolk, one-half cup milk, one tablespoonful sugar, pinch of salt, nutmeg. Beat egg and sugar, heat milk, pour over egg, cook in double boiler till it coats the spoon, about five minutes. Bake in a buttered dish, eight minutes in slow oven.

QUINCE HONEY.

Four quinces, three apples grated raw, four pounds sugar and one pint water cooked together, then put in the quinces and apples and boil twenty minutes.

SAILOR'S DUFF.

One egg and two tablespoonfuls sugar, beaten together, and one-half cup molasses beaten in. Then add two tablespoonfuls melted butter and beat again; one teaspoonful soda dissolved in a little warm water, one and one-half cup fine white pastry flour, one-half cup boiling water, added last. Steam three-fourths of an hour.

SAUCE.

Yolks of two eggs, add one cup pulverized sugar and one teaspoonful vanilla extract, well beaten together; add one-half pint whipped cream just before serving.

SAUCE FOR ICE CREAM.

To six figs add a pint of hot water. When they have cooked a short time, add enough granulated sugar to make a rich syrup and stew them until the figs are tender. After they are cold, add a tablespoonful of vanilla. Pour over the ice cream. Serve in glass cups and add a portion of the fig on each cup.

SNOW PUDDING.

Soak one tablespoonful gelatine in one-fourth cup cold water, add a little pinch of salt, and dissolve in one and one-fourth cup boiling water; add three-fourths cup sugar and one-fourth cup lemon juice. When mixture begins to form, beat with a Dover beater until almost white, then add well-beaten whites of three eggs and beat thoroughly. Set aside to cool, and serve with sweet or whipped cream.

SNOW CUSTARD.

One-half package of Cox's gelatine, three eggs, two cups sugar, one large cup boiling water, one pint milk, juice of one lemon. Soak the gelatine one hour in a teacupful of cold water. Then stir in two-thirds of the sugar, the lemon juice and the boiling water. Beat the whites of the eggs to a stiff froth, and when the strained gelatine is quite cold, whip it into the whites, a spoonful at a time—for half an hour if you use the Dover egg beater, at least an hour with any other. When all is white and stiff, pour into a wet mold. Make the custard of the sugar, yolks and milk; flavor with vanilla. Boil until it begins to thicken. When the meringue is turned into the dish, pour the cold custard about the base.

SNOWBALLS.

Three eggs, one scant cup flour, one cup sugar, one and one-half teaspoonful baking powder, three tablespoonfuls water, two tablespoonfuls lemon juice, grated rind of one lemon. Beat yolks of eggs, add sugar, then water, lemon rind and juice, then the whites beaten stiffly, finally the flour and baking powder, sifted together. Stir quickly and well. Pour this batter into fifteen little, well-buttered cups, steam one-half hour, have three tablespoonfuls powdered sugar on a plate. When snowballs are done, turn out on the sugar; roll them till covered with sugar. Serve with Strawberry Sauce:

STRAWBERRY SAUCE.

One can strawberries, put enough strawberries through a sieve to make one-half cup. Stir this into whipped cream which has been thoroughly chilled.

SPANISH CREAM.

One lemon, two eggs, one tablespoonful butter. Beat sugar and butter together, then add eggs. Grate rind of lemon and squeeze out juice, add last and bake five minutes.

SPONGE PUDDING.

One-half cup flour, dissolved in a little more than one pint milk. Set into a pan of water and boil until thick. Stir into this mixture while warm one teaspoonful butter. Separate whites and yolks of six eggs and add the yolks, well beaten, one-half cup granulated sugar, then beat well again. Beat white to stiff froth and stir all into the thickened milk, whites last. Bake one hour in pudding pan placed in hot water. Serve with cream, lightly whipped and flavored with vanilla.

STEAMED PRUNE PUDDING.

One-third cup stale bread crumbs, one-third cup fine chopped suet, one-third cup prune puree, one level teaspoonful baking powder, one egg beaten light, one-third cup flour, one-third cup sugar, one-fourth teaspoonful salt, one-third cup milk. Recipe for ten people.

STEAM PUDDING.

Beat yolks of three eggs, add one cup sugar, three tablespoonfuls milk; beat thoroughly, add one ounce melted chocolate, one cup flour, beaten whites of three eggs, with two tablespoonfuls baking powder; steam thirty minutes. Makes eight cups pudding. Grease cups.

SAUCE FOR SAME.

One-half cup sugar to one cup water, one-fourth cup flour, one tablespoonful butter. Mix flour and sugar together, add flavoring, boil in double boiler until thick like custard.

SUET PUDDING.

Two cups flour, two and one-half teaspoonfuls baking powder, a little salt, four eggs, whites and yolks beaten separately, one and one-half cup sweet milk, one cup suet chopped fine, two cups raisins well floured. Put in mold or bag and boil about two hours. This is a nice, simple pudding.

SUET PUDDING.

One cup suet, one pound raisins, one and one-half cup milk, one cup sugar, cinnamon, cloves, nutmeg, two large teaspoonfuls baking powder; thicken with cracker crumbs, but not too stiff. Steam three hours. Serve with hard sauce.

TAPIOCA PUDDING.

Four tablespoonfuls tapioca, one quart milk, four eggs (leaving out the whites of two for frosting), three tablespoonfuls sugar. Soak the tapioca over night, or for several hours (four will do) in enough water to cover it. Let the milk come to a boil and pour over the tapioca. When it cools to blood-warm, add the sugar, then the eggs, well beaten. Bake about an hour in a moderate oven. Take out, and when it has cooled a little, spread over the top the whites of the two eggs whipped stiff and one-half cup powdered sugar added. Return to top shelf for about two minutes, or until the frosting is browned.

WOODFORD PUDDING.

Three eggs, one cup sugar, one cup flour, one cup jam, one teaspoonful soda dissolved in three tablespoonfuls sour milk, cinnamon and nutmeg to taste. Pour batter into greased cake pan and steam over boiling water three hours. For the sauce, whites of three eggs and one cup sugar, beaten together, one teaspoonful vanilla, and when ready to serve add one pint cream, well beaten.

CAKE

"Have I not earned my cake in baking it?" — Tennyson.

ALDEN OATMEAL COOKIES.

Cream one and one-half cup butter with two cups brown sugar, add three well-beaten eggs, one-half cup milk (sweet or sour), one and one-half teaspoonful soda, one and one-half teaspoonful cinnamon, three cups uncooked oatmeal and three cups flour, one pound raisins chopped fine. Drop by spoonfuls on greased pans.

ANGEL FOOD.

Whites of twelve eggs, one-half pint flour, three-fourths pint sugar, one level teaspoonful cream of tartar. Beat the whites to a stiff froth. Sift the sugar and flour separately four times before measuring. Add the cream of tartar to the flour after measuring and sift once more. Add the sugar to the eggs and last the flour. Do not grease the pan. Bake forty minutes in a moderate oven.

BLACK CAKE.

One cup sugar, one-half cup butter, three eggs beaten separately, one cup cold black coffee or milk, one-half cup grated chocolate, one and one-half cup flour, two teaspoonfuls baking powder, a little cloves and cinnamon and a pinch of salt.

BOSTON CAKE.

One pound sugar, one pound flour, one-half pound butter, four eggs, one nutmeg, one-half pound raisins, one teacup sweet milk, one teaspoonful soda, one wineglassful brandy or wine, one teaspoonful cinnamon, one-half teaspoonful cloves. The above recipe can be modified by using coffee instead of milk, and a couple of teaspoonfuls of baking powder instead of soda, leaving out the raisins.

½-1-2-3-4 CAKE.

One-half cup butter, large; one cup milk, two cups sugar, three cups flour, four eggs and three teaspoonfuls baking powder. This can be used as a layer cake, or nuts or raisins can be added.

CALIFORNIA COOKIES.

Two cups sugar, one cup butter and lard melted, four cups flour, two-thirds cup sweet milk, three teaspoonfuls baking powder, one-half nutmeg, one egg. Mix as for ordinary cake, roll thin, put raisins or salted almonds in center of each and bake a light brown.

CALIFORNIA WHITE CAKE.

One cup granulated sugar, one-fourth cup butter, one and one-half cup flour, one-half cup sweet milk, one and one-half teaspoonful baking powder, whites of three eggs beaten stiff, flavoring. Bake in two layers.

CARAMEL FILLING.

One pint brown sugar, one-half cup milk, one tablespoonful butter, one teaspoonful vanilla. Boil to a syrup.

CHARLOTTE RUSSE SPONGE CAKE.

One cup sugar, four eggs, four tablespoonfuls water, one and one-half cup flour, one teaspoonful baking powder, flavor to taste.

FILLING.

One-half pint cream flavor and add a pinch of gelatine dissolved in hot water. You may use two and one-half times recipe.

CHOCOLATE ICING.

Whites of three eggs, one cup sugar, one-half pint grated chocolate.

COCOANUT CAKE.

Whites of four eggs, one-half teacup butter, one teacup sugar, one teacup sweet milk, two cups flour, two teaspoonfuls cream of tartar, one teaspoonful soda, flavor with lemon. Bake in jelly cake pans. When done, have ready icing made not quite so stiff as for the tops of cake; three eggs will make enough. Spread the layers with icing. Sprinkle quite thick with cocoanut.

COOKIES.

One and one-half cup sugar, one cup butter, three eggs, four cups flour, one teaspoonful soda in a little hot water, one cup chopped walnut meats, one cup chopped raisins. Cream the sugar and butter; add the eggs, well beaten, then the flour, nuts and raisins, last the soda. Drop on buttered pan and bake in hot oven.

COOKIES.

Two scant cups sugar, two eggs, one-half cup sour cream or sour milk, one teaspoonful soda, season with nutmeg, flour enough to roll out.

CREAM COOKIES.

One cup sour cream, one cup shortening, two cups sugar, one teaspoonful soda, one tablespoonful lemon extract, three eggs.

CREAM CAKE.

Yolk of four eggs, one cup granulated sugar, beat very well; four tablespoonfuls hot water, add one-half cup sifted flour, one and one-half teaspoonful baking powder, four beaten whites, moderate oven, flavor, three yolks eggs, three tablespoonfuls sugar, one pint milk, pinch of salt, one and one-half teaspoonful cornstarch, flavor.

CUP CAKE.

One cup butter, two cups sugar, three cups flour, four eggs, scant cup water, two heaping teaspoonfuls baking powder.

DOUGHNUTS.

One cup sugar, yolks of four eggs, one cup sour milk, one teaspoonful soda, nutmeg and pinch of cinnamon, pinch salt, two large spoonfuls melted butter, flour enough to roll out.

DOUGHNUTS.

Cream together one teaspoonful butter, one cup sugar. Beat into them one egg, one-half teaspoonful salt and grated nutmeg, two teaspoonfuls baking powder, one quart flour sifted together, one cup milk; add alternately to make a soft dough. Do not knead. Roll one-half inch thick, cut out, fry in lard.

DUTCH CAKES.

One-half pint milk, one-half pint warm water, one-half cake yeast, one heaping tablespoonful sugar, one teaspoonful salt, one egg. Flour enough to make a soft dough. Let rise in warm place two or three hours until light, then roll one-half inch thick, cut into two-inch squares, let rise again one-half hour and fry in hot lard just as you do doughnuts.

EXCELLENT GINGERBREAD.

One cup brown sugar, one-half cup butter, four eggs, one cup sour cream or milk, one cup New Orleans molasses, three cups flour, one teaspoonful allspice, one teaspoonful cloves, one teaspoonful ginger, two tablespoonfuls cinnamon, one teaspoonful soda. This will make two sheets. Bake in moderate oven.

ENGLISH WALNUT CAKE.

One cup butter, two cups sugar, one cup milk, three cups flour; three eggs, both whites and yolks beaten thoroughly together; two teaspoonfuls baking powder, one cup English walnuts chopped fine. For the icing use the whites of three eggs and one pound confectioners' sugar, flavored with vanilla. Bake the batter in two dripping pans about fifteen inches long and six inches wide. When cold, cut each in half, spread icing between, then ice the tops; with a knife mark off squares, and lay one-half out each square. As there are often poor nuts among the good, it is best to have one and one-half pound on hand.

EGG KISSES.

Whites of four eggs, one pint granulated sugar. Beat with silver spoon for forty minutes, add nut kernels and drop from spoon on buttered papers. Bake in slow oven on inverted bread pans.

FEATHER CAKE.

One-half cup butter, two cups sugar, three cups flour, one cup sweet milk, three eggs, two teaspoonfuls baking powder, grated rind of lemon. Bake in long pan. Sprinkle top with sugar. Cut slices out of pan when served.

FLORIDA DOUGHNUTS.

Three eggs, one cup sugar, one tablespoonful butter, one teaspoonful soda, two teaspoonfuls cream of tartar dissolved in one cup milk, flour to roll.

FRENCH CREAM CAKE.

Three eggs, one cup granulated sugar, one and one-half cup flour, four tablespoonfuls cold water, one teaspoonful baking powder. This is enough for two cakes, baked in pie pans, to be split while warm, spreading the hot custard between them. For custard, boil nearly one pint sweet milk, mix two tablespoonfuls cornstarch with a half teacup sweet milk, add two well-beaten eggs; when milk has boiled, add nearly a cup sugar, and add gradually the cornstarch and eggs, stirring briskly; add a half cup butter, stirring until dissolved. Flavor with one teaspoonful vanilla and spread between cakes while hot.

GERMAN COFFEE CAKE.

Three cups flour, one-half teaspoonful salt, three tablespoonfuls sugar, two teaspoonfuls baking powder. Rub in two tablespoonfuls butter, beat two eggs, two-thirds cup sweet milk; add more milk if necessary to make stiff batter. Spread in pan, mix together two tablespoonfuls flour, four tablespoonfuls sugar, one heaping tablespoonful cinnamon or chocolate. Rub in tablespoonful butter until crumbly, spread thickly over top of dough and bake one-half hour.

GINGER BREAD.

One-half cup of butter or lard, one-half cup sugar, two eggs, one cup molasses, two and one-half cups flour, one teaspoonful ginger, one teaspoonful cinnamon, one-half teaspoonful cloves, one-fourth teaspoonful salt, two teaspoonfuls baking soda dissolved in boiling water, last.

GOLDEN CAKE.

Yolks of eight eggs, one-half cup butter, two cups sugar, four cups flour, one cup milk, three tablespoonfuls baking powder. Mix butter and sugar, add flour and milk, then yolks well beaten.

GRANDMOTHER'S SPONGE CAKE.

One pound sugar (leave a little out for top of cake), one-half pound flour, the grated rind and juice of one lemon, twelve eggs (leaving out the yolks of eight of the eggs). Beat the yolks (four) light, then add sugar and beat very hard. Mix in the flour and part of the whites very slowly. Bake from one and one-half to two hours.

HERMITS.

One and one-half cup sugar, one cup butter, three eggs (whites and yolks beaten separately), one teaspoonful cinnamon, one teaspoonful ginger, one teaspoonful allspice, one teaspoonful cloves, one nutmeg, juice of lemon, one cup raisins (stone and pull in pieces), two teaspoonfuls baking powder, trifle over three cups flour.

HICKORY NUT CAKE.

Stir one cup of butter and two of granulated sugar to a cream. Beat the whites of six eggs to a stiff froth. Sift flour, then measure four cups and add to it two teaspoonfuls baking powder. Sift again, three times. Now stir in the creamed butter and sugar, one cup sweet milk and most of the flour, a little at a time, alternately. Then balance of flour and egg. Don't beat, only stir well and lightly. Bake in *moderate* oven. When you add milk and flour, stir in one cup of hickory nuts, chopped tolerably fine and floured.

ICING.

Whites of five eggs, one and one-fourth pound powdered sugar, teaspoonful vanilla, a tiny bit of citric acid. Put all the sugar except two ounces in a bright tin pan with just enough water to moisten well. Place on stove to boil. While this is boiling beat eggs to a stiff froth, then add the two ounces of sugar, a little at a time. Now try the boiling syrup in cold water, as for taffy, and when brittle pour in a fine stream into the eggs previously prepared, beating hard all the time. Beat awhile and while cooling add vanilla and citric acid. When nearly cold spread on cake.

JAM CAKE.

One cup blackberry jam, one cup sugar, three cups flour, one-half cup butter, one-half cup sour milk, one teaspoonful soda, four eggs (two will do, if scarce), one teaspoonful of all kinds of spices and nutmeg.

KISMET CAKE.

Butterless, Eggless and Milkless Cake.

One-half cup brown sugar, one cup water, one-third cup pork drippings, one pound seeded raisins, one-half teaspoonful nutmeg, one teaspoonful cinnamon, three-fourths teaspoonful cloves, one-half teaspoonful salt. Boil together five minutes. Cool, and then add one teaspoonful baking soda, dissolved in one-half cup hot water; then two cups flour, in which one-half teaspoonful of baking powder has been sifted. Bake in a moderate oven.

LADY BALTIMORE CAKE.

One cup butter, two cups sugar, three and one-half cups flour, one cup sweet milk, whites of six eggs, two level teaspoonfuls baking powder. Bake in three layers.

FILLING.

Three cups granulated sugar dissolved in boiling water. Cook until it threads, then pour slowly over beaten whites of three more eggs, stirring constantly. Add to this frosting one cup chopped raisins, one cup pecans and five figs cut in very thin, small slices. Spread at once over layers, top and sides of cake.

MARSHMALLOW ICING.

Two cups granulated sugar, one cup milk; cook these together until it strings. Melt one-fourth pound (or twenty) marshmallows by steaming them after putting three tablespoonfuls boiling water over them. Add to cream filling and beat until stiff enough to spread.

MRS. AULTMAN'S COOKIES.

Two cups sugar, one cup butter or lard, five eggs, three teaspoonfuls baking powder; mix stiff enough to roll. Bake in moderate oven.

NUT CAKE.

One cup sugar, one-half cup butter, two eggs, one-half cup water, one and one-half cup flour, one-half teaspoonful cream of tartar, one cup chopped hickory nuts. Ice the top, place on large pieces of English walnuts.

OATMEAL COOKIES.

Two cups rolled oats, two cups flour, one cup sugar, one cup raisins, one cup lard and butter mixed, two eggs, one teaspoonful cloves, one teaspoonful cinnamon, three-fourths teaspoonful baking soda dissolved in one-third cup milk, a little salt. Mix thoroughly and drop on greased pans. Bake in moderate oven.

PRESBYTERIAN COOKIES.

Four eggs, one cup of butter (or Crisco), two cups light brown sugar, three rounded teaspoonfuls baking powder, two teaspoonfuls extract lemon or vanilla, flour to make dough of medium consistency. Roll not too thin, bake in hot oven. Makes fifty cookies.

QUICK COFFEE CAKE.

Sift together twice one cup flour, one-half cup cornstarch, one-third cup sugar, three level teaspoonfuls baking powder, a little salt and one-half teaspoonful ground cinnamon. Mix to a soft dough with about one-half cup milk stirred into a well-beaten egg. Add four tablespoonfuls melted butter, spread in a shallow pan, sprinkle with sugar mixed with cinnamon, and bake in a moderate oven.

ROCK COOKIES.

One cup dates, one cup figs, one cup English or common walnuts, one and one-half cup brown sugar, one-half cup butter, one teaspoonful cinnamon, one-half teaspoonful allspice, one tablespoonful baking soda dissolved in one tablespoonful boiling water, two eggs, three cups flour. Mix well and drop from a spoon on to a well-greased pan, and bake in a slow oven. Cut nuts, figs and dates in small pieces.

SILVER CAKE.

Whites of four eggs, three-fourths cup sugar, one-half cup butter, one and one-half cup flour, one-third cup sweet milk, one teaspoonful baking powder, one-half teaspoonful lemon juice. Cream butter and sugar, then add eggs, then milk. Add flour next, then baking powder and, last, flavoring. Bake in moderate oven.

To make a gold cake use the same recipe as for silver cake, substituting yolks for whites of eggs, and vanilla in place of lemon juice.

SHIPMAN'S GINGER BREAD.

One cup sugar, one cup molasses, one-half cup butter, one cup sour milk, three and one-half cups flour, three eggs, one heaped teaspoonful ginger, one even teaspoonful salt, one tablespoonful cinnamon, one tablespoonful saleratus, stirred in dry. If milk is sweet, stir in one tablespoonful vinegar and set it on the stove until it sours.

SOFT GINGER COOKIES.

One-half cup brown sugar, one cup New Orleans molasses, one-half cup sour milk, one-half cup butter, one tablespoonful ginger, one tablespoonful cinnamon, one teaspoonful soda, two eggs, enough flour to make a dough stiff enough to roll out, cut with cutter and bake in moderate oven.

SPICE CAKE.

Two cups sugar, one cup butter, one cup milk, five eggs, three cups flour, two teaspoonfuls baking powder, one teaspoonful cinnamon, allspice, cloves and nutmeg, one cup raisins if desired.

SPICE CAKE.

One and one-half cup granulated sugar, one-half cup butter, one-half cup milk, three eggs (whites beaten separately), three cups flour, two teaspoonfuls baking powder, two teaspoonfuls cinnamon, one teaspoonful allspice, one pound raisins, cut fine and well floured.

SPONGE CAKE.

Seven eggs, separate yolks and whites, beat the whites to a stiff froth; three cups powdered sugar, beaten well with the yolks, three cups flour and one cup water, again well beaten with the sugar and yolks; three level teaspoonfuls baking powder and the whites of the eggs, previously well beaten to a stiff froth, laid over the top of the sponge, and all well beaten for five minutes. Bake in a slow oven.

SPONGE CAKE.

Eleven eggs, four cups powdered sugar, four cups flour, one cup cold water, omit yolks of two eggs, beat nine yolks lightly and add sugar and water gradually, add whites, also beaten until very light, then stir in the flour, in the last cupful of which put one large teaspoonful baking powder and one-half teaspoonful salt.

SPONGE CAKE.

Four eggs, two cups powdered sugar, two cups flour, three-fourths cup very hot water, two teaspoonfuls baking powder, one-half teaspoonful salt. Cream yolks of eggs and sugar, add one-half the hot water; mix flour, salt, and baking powder, and alternate with the hot water. Beat whites of eggs to a stiff froth and add to mixture. Flavor to taste. Bake in moderate oven.

SPONGE CAKE.

Place upon the stove one cup milk and two tablespoonfuls butter. Beat four eggs light with two cups sugar, stir in two cups flour, two teaspoonfuls baking powder, then add hot milk and butter and flavoring. Beat thoroughly and bake in a loaf in a moderate oven.

SPRINGERS.

Four eggs well beaten, one pound powdered sugar, one pound flour, a pinch of salt, one-eighth teaspoonful soda, flavor with anise.

SUNSHINE CAKE.

Whites of seven eggs, yolks of five eggs, one and one-fourth cup granulated sugar, one cup flour, one-fourth teaspoonful cream of tartar, one teaspoonful lemon and orange extract. Beat whites of eggs very stiff, adding cream of tartar while beating. Beat yolks until lemon color. Sift sugar and flour several times before measuring. For mixing add beaten yolks to beaten whites and fold in the sugar and flour alternately; do not beat, only stir enough to mix thoroughly, and add extract last. Bake in Van Duzen pan forty-five minutes in a moderate oven.

TOLEDO CUP CAKE.

One-fourth cup butter, one-half cup sugar, one-fourth cup milk, one egg, one small cup flour, one teaspoonful baking powder, one-half teaspoonful vanilla. Rub the butter and sugar to a cream, beat the egg light without separating and put it in next, then the milk, a little at a time. Add the baking powder and flour, and then the vanilla. Bake in little tins.

VELVET SPONGE CAKE.

Two cups sugar, six eggs, leaving out the whites of three, one cup boiling water, two and one-half cups flour, two teaspoonfuls baking powder in the flour; beat the yolks a little, add the sugar and beat fifteen minutes; add the three beaten whites and the cup of boiling water just before the flour; flavor with a teaspoonful lemon extract and bake in three layers, putting between them icing made by adding to the three whites of eggs beaten to a stiff froth six dessert-spoonfuls pulverized sugar to each egg, and lemon to flavor.

WHITE ICING.

Four cups sugar, one-half teaspoonful cream of tartar, one-half teaspoonful baking powder, one cup hot water, whites of four eggs, juice of one-half lemon. Mix sugar, cream of tartar and baking powder. Add water and let boil. Do not stir. Beat whites of eggs, standing in a pan of hot water. Add boiling syrup, a spoonful at a time, slowly, until half has been added. Put in lemon juice and beat hard, letting the rest of the syrup boil until it looks thick. Then pour it into mixture, beating hard. Set in pan over hot water until it will stand alone when dropped from spoon. If not thick enough, beat and steam again; if too thick, add boiling water and steam more.

WHITE MOUNTAIN CAKE.

Two cups pulverized sugar, one-half cup butter beaten to a cream; add one-half cup sweet milk, two and one-half cups flour, two and one-half teaspoonfuls baking powder in the flour, whites of eight eggs; bake in jelly tins and put together with icing made by boiling one-half teacup water and three teacups sugar till thick; pour it slowly over the well-beaten whites of three eggs and beat all together till cool. Beat before putting on each layer. Sprinkle each layer thickly with grated cocoanut, and a handsome cocoanut cake will result.

WHITE PERFECTION CAKE.

Three cups sugar, one cup butter, one cup milk, three cups flour, one cup cornstarch, three teaspoonfuls baking powder, whites of twelve eggs beaten to a stiff froth, cream, sugar and butter; dissolve cornstarch in milk and add to the sugar and butter; mix flour and baking powder and add to mixture. Lastly the whites of eggs, well beaten. Bake in a moderate oven.

FRUITS

Fruit of all kinds
She gathers, tribute large, and on the board
Heaps with unsparing hand.—Milton.

APPLES.

While most people prefer apples cooked in some form, they are very good and wholesome when eaten raw. There are so many varieties of this fruit that one finds flavors of almost all other fruits if one tastes a number of different kinds of apples.

BANANAS.

This is a fruit which is delicious eaten in almost any form. It is especially good frozen.

CANTALOUPES.

Cantaloupes should be kept on ice and served in halves, each half filled with chopped ice or peaches, as a breakfast dish. To clean cantaloupes, scrape out seeds and wash out each half under the cold-water faucet. The half may be filled with ice cream and served as a dessert.

GRAPES.

Put bunches in a colander and pour cold water over them. Drain and chill, and arrange prettily on dish. Always be sure to remove the imperfect grapes.

GRAPE FRUIT.

(SHADDOCK.)

This fruit was named for Captain Shaddock, who first brought it from the East Indies. It is delicious, and supposed to have medicinal value. It is refreshing served for breakfast, but may be used as first course for any meal. It should be prepared several hours before needed. Cut in half, remove center pulp with scissors or sharp, small knife; cut each section away from pulp, put two tablespoonfuls powdered sugar and a Maraschino cherry in center of each half. Place in cool place till ready to serve.

ORANGES.

Oranges are the most delightful eaten raw, but there are many other ways of serving them, the Seville orange being the most preferable for cooking, and is a little bitter. A simple way of preparing them for a dessert is to peel the oranges so as to remove outer layer of pulp, then remove each section from pulp. Put alternately into dessert dish a layer of oranges sprinkled with powdered sugar and a layer of shredded cocoanut. Place in cool place and serve.

PEACHES AND PEARS.

These fruits have the high esteem of many people in warm and temperate climates. The peach is called the Persian apple, and is, like the pear, delicious served either cooked or raw.

STRAWBERRIES.

These are best served raw, and may be hulled, or if cream is not desired, serve with the hulls left on and put a mound of powdered sugar in the center of the fruit dishes.

PICKLES AND PRESERVES

"Touch you the sourest points with sweetest terms." —Shakespeare.

CATSUP.

To one bushel tomatoes use one small measure onions; boil and sift; one handful salt, one tablespoonful mustard, one tablespoonful cayenne pepper, two tablespoonfuls black pepper, one-half pound sugar. Add spice just before it is finished boiling.

CHILI SAUCE.

Twelve large, ripe tomatoes, two onions, two green peppers, two tablespoonfuls salt, one cup sugar, one cup vinegar, one teaspoonful each cinnamon, allspice, cloves; chop fine, boil about two hours.

CHILI SAUCE.

One peck ripe tomatoes, twelve large onions, four cups vinegar, six tablespoonfuls salt, twelve large tablespoonfuls sugar, four red mango peppers, ground cloves, cinnamon, allspice and nutmeg to taste; chop onions and peppers fine; cut tomatoes in small pieces and drain. Boil all things half an hour. Put in sealed jars.

CUCUMBER PICKLE.

Place the cucumber in a stone jar. Make a strong brine, strong enough to bear up an egg; pour it over them boiling hot, let them stand over night, in the morning pour off the brine and wipe the cucumbers dry, put them in a preserving kettle and pour over them enough cider-vinegar to cover them; put in also the following spices for four hundred pickles: Two ounces whole cloves, two tablespoonfuls white mustard seed, several strips horseradish, four or five sticks cinnamon, coffee-cupful brown sugar, two ounces allspice, four small red peppers cut in small pieces and the seed taken out, three onions sliced. Let all come to a boil, boil for five minutes, and put boiling hot over cucumbers.

CUCUMBER SWEET PICKLES.

Put small cucumbers in a dish with one-half cup salt to two quarts cucumbers; cover with boiling water and let stand all night. Remove from brine, place in granite kettle, cover with vinegar containing whole mustard seed, cloves and cinnamon and one cup of sugar. Let come to boiling point, but not boil. Can, or bottle while hot.

FRENCH PICKLE.

One peck green tomatoes sliced, six large onions sliced; mix these and throw over them one teacupful of salt, let them stand over night; next day drain thoroughly, boil in one quart of vinegar mixed with two quarts of water for fifteen minutes, then drain; take four quarts vinegar, two pounds brown sugar, two tablespoonfuls cinnamon, mace, cloves; tie spices in little bags, put all together and boil ten or fifteen minutes.

GERMAN PICKLED PLUMS OR PEACHES.

One pint vinegar, seven pounds plums or peaches, three pounds sugar, one ounce cinnamon (whole), one ounce cloves (whole), a layer of plums, layer of spice, layer of sugar. Have your vinegar scalded and pour over the plums, going through this process for three successive days. Put all in a kettle and let them come to a boil, and they are ready for use.

GREEN TOMATO PICKLE.

Twelve green tomatoes, three large onions. Boil in salt and water and drain, or sprinkle with salt and allow it to stand all night, then drain. Scald in vinegar to which has been added one cup of brown sugar, one stick of cinnamon bark, a few cloves, red pepper to taste.

SPICED GRAPES.

Seven pounds grapes, one pint vinegar, three and one-half pounds sugar (or more if you like), one-half ounce ground cloves, one-half ounce ground cinnamon. Slip the pulp out of the skins, scald it, then pass through a sieve to seed. Then put the juice and skins and all the seasoning together and boil fifteen minutes.

SWEET PICKLE BEETS.

Boil the beets till they can be pierced with a fork; put into cold water, slip off the skins and slice. Boil one quart of vinegar, two cups brown sugar, add sliced beets, a little salt and pepper, boil five or ten minutes, place in cans and close tightly.

UNCOOKED SWEET PICKLES (300).

As pickles are often put up in very warm weather, this recipe will be found especially simple and easy to carry out.

One gallon cider vinegar, one cup granulated sugar, one-third cup salt, one cup freshly grated horseradish (or two five-cent glasses), one-half cup ground mustard, one-third ounce saccharine, two tablespoonfuls mixed spices in each quart jar. Be sure to get in a few red peppers and cloves. Put pickles in jars and fill with above mixture, cold.

PRESERVES AND JELLIES

BLACKBERRY JAM.

Press the berries through a colander, add one pound brown sugar to a pint of juice. Let it boil slowly more than half a day.

CHERRY PRESERVES.

Wash the cherries, pick and stone them, then weigh, taking the same amount of sugar as cherries. Let them stand one hour, put on fire and let them boil through thoroughly. Pour on a flat platter and let them stand in the sun until they thicken.

CRAB-APPLE JELLY.

Wash apples, remove blossom and stem ends, put them whole into a porcelain-lined preserving kettle, add cold water to nearly cover apples, cover and cook slowly until soft. Mash and drain through cheese-cloth or coarse sieve. It makes the jelly cloudy to squeeze the apples. Now allow juice to drip through a jelly bag or through two thicknesses of cheese-cloth, boil twenty minutes and add equal quantity of sugar, boil five minutes, skim and turn in glasses. Let the glasses stand in a sunny window twenty-four hours. A sprig of rose geranium dropped in syrup while it is boiling the last time will give the jelly a delicious and unusual flavor.

CURRANT AND RASPBERRY PRESERVES.

Pick over six pounds of currants, wash and drain, put into a preserving kettle a few at a time and mash, cook an hour and strain through double thickness of cheese-cloth. Then return to kettle, add six pounds of sugar, bring to boiling point and cook slowly twenty minutes. Bring syrup to boil again, add one quart of raspberries, skim out raspberries, put in jar, and repeat until raspberries are used. Fill jars with syrup, and screw on tops.

GRAPE JELLY.

Wild grapes make the best jelly, though the other kind are more frequently used. Pick them over, wash and remove stems, put into kettle, heat to boiling point, mash and boil thirty minutes, strain through coarse strainer, then allow juice to drip through a double thickness of cheese-cloth. Measure and boil for five minutes, add equal quantity of heated sugar, boil three minutes, skim and pour into glasses. Stand in sunny window twenty-four hours, cover and keep in cool, dry place.

MARMALADE.

One grapefruit, one orange, one lemon; shave these fine, add five times as much water, let stand over night, then boil ten minutes; let stand until next morning. Add the same quantity of sugar as fruit. Cook until it jellies, and put in glasses.

PLUM COMPOTE.

For this delicious sweet, take six pounds pitted plums (Damson), six pounds granulated sugar, one pound seeded raisins, four large oranges chopped, one pound shelled English walnuts or pecans. Boil to consistency of jelly: Nuts are added just before taking off fire. Roll oranges before removing the rind. Put oranges and juice, also sugar, on the plums and let stand over night. Stir often.

RED RASPBERRY JAM.

One-third red currants, two-thirds raspberries, three-fourths pound sugar to a pound of fruit. Boil until done.

CANDIES

"Yet to my raised imagination, divested of its homelier qualities,
it appeared a glorified candy." — Lamb.

BUTTER SCOTCH.

Two cups sugar, two tablespoonfuls water, butter size of egg. Boil without stirring until it hardens on a spoon; pour out on buttered plates to cool.

CHOCOLATE FUDGE.

Two cups sugar, one-fourth cake Baker's bitter chocolate, one cup milk, butter size of an egg, vanilla to flavor. Scrape chocolate, add sugar, milk and butter. Boil until a ball can be formed with fingers in a little cold water. Beat in vanilla, beat until quite stiff. Put in buttered platter. A cup of chopped nuts may be added, if desired.

COCOANUT FUDGE.

Two cups sugar, one cup milk, one box desiccated cocoanut, small lump butter. Cook sugar, milk and butter fifteen minutes, take off the fire, and beat with a spoon. When partly creamed, add cocoanut and one teaspoonful vanilla. Stir well, pour into buttered pan and cut in squares.

CREAM FUDGE.

Two cups sugar, one cup milk, small lump butter. Cook fifteen minutes, set pan in a cool place, and when about half cooled beat with a spoon. Pour when creamy into buttered pan and cut when still warm into squares. Vanilla or any other flavoring improves this fudge.

FONDANT.

Two cups sugar, nine tablespoonfuls water; when it begins to boil, put in one-fourth teaspoonful cream of tartar; do not stir after it begins to boil: In four minutes try by dropping in water; if it balls, take off the stove and let it cool until it wrinkles on top when moved; then stir until you can mold it with the hand. Put in flavor and coloring after you mold it. This will make any kind of candy by using nuts and flavors of different kinds. Lay on greased paper.

FUDGE.

One and one-half pound granulated sugar (equal to three cups), one cup cream, one-half teaspoonful salt; put in saucepan and boil. Nuts, three squares bitter chocolate (Baker's). One heaping tablespoonful butter, one teaspoonful flavoring; cut up cup marshmallows in little squares.

ICE CREAM CANDY.

One pound granulated sugar, one pound pulverized sugar, one cup water, two tablespoonfuls white vinegar, one teaspoonful glycerine. Put all in saucepan; when it begins to boil, quit stirring, put in flavoring, then one-half teaspoonful cream of tartar. After it stops boiling, cool off a little, then pull, lay out on marble slab, cut in squares.

MAPLE CREAM FUDGE.

One and three-fourths cup sugar, three-fourths cup milk, one-third cup maple syrup, butter size of an egg. Mix all ingredients together in an enameled saucepan, boil about ten minutes, beat until almost stiff and pour into buttered platter, mark into squares while warm. Cocoanut or chopped nuts, added while beating, makes a variety.

MEXICAN CANDY.

Two cups brown sugar, one cup granulated sugar, three-fourths teaspoonful cream of tartar, one tablespoonful butter, one teaspoonful vanilla, one-half pound pecans cut in coarse pieces. Boil to a soft state, add butter and vanilla.

MOLASSES CANDY.

One cup molasses, one cup sugar, one tablespoonful vinegar, small lump butter; cook until it hardens in water; pour out, and when cool pull until a light yellow.

PEANUT BUTTER FUDGE.

Two heaping tablespoonfuls of peanut butter, scant teaspoonful of salt, two cups sugar, one cup milk. Put sugar and milk in saucepan, stir them, add the peanut butter and salt. Stir occasionally while cooking. Should be cooked slowly until a soft ball can be formed if dropped into cup of cold water. Beat vigorously until it begins to stiffen, then pour in butter platter. This makes a delicious, creamy candy, if beaten enough.

PEANUT CANDY.

Two cups brown sugar, one tablespoonful molasses, one teaspoonful vinegar, lump butter. Cook until it hardens in water, and pour over peanuts placed in buttered pans.

PEANUT TAFFY.

Two cups granulated sugar put into a hot spider over a good fire and stirred constantly until entirely dissolved. Use no water. First the sugar will become lumpy, and it will not seem possible that it will become liquid, but patience and constant stirring will produce the desired result. When melted about like molasses, add one cup chopped peanuts and pour quickly into a greased platter. It requires experience to gain best results.

PRALINE.

Three cups brown sugar, one cup water, one cup cream, one cup nuts cut fine, one teaspoonful vanilla. Boil sugar and water until it forms a soft ball, add cream and boil until it forms a soft ball, stirring constantly after adding cream. When cooked enough, beat in the nuts and drop on a greased pan.

SEA FOAM.

Two cups brown sugar, one-half cup water. Boil until it forms a soft ball; add one-half cup nuts cut fine and a little vanilla. Beat until it creams up; drop on greased pan or paper.

TAFFY.

Two cups granulated sugar, one cup water, one tablespoonful water, one tablespoonful vinegar, butter size of a walnut, and a pinch of salt. Boil without stirring till it forms a ball when dropped into cold water. Flavor with vanilla when almost pulled.

WHITE PULLED CANDY.

Two cups sugar, one cup water, one tablespoonful vinegar, one teaspoonful butter. Cook until it hardens in water, pour out, and when cool pull until white.

MISCELLANEOUS

BAKED CHEESE.

Three eggs, one cup bread crumbs, one pint milk (or little over), one-half cup grated cheese, lump of butter size of walnut, pepper and salt to taste. Soak the bread crumbs in the milk fifteen or twenty minutes. Then stir with that the beaten eggs, butter, etc. Put into a buttered baking dish and bake about thirty minutes.

BAKING POWDER.

One pound cream of tartar, one-half pound bicarbonate of soda, one-half pound flour. Sift the soda and flour together several times, then mix in cream of tartar and sift again. Put in glass jar and keep dry.

BANANA FRITTERS.

Prepare batter as for plain fritters. Into this dip the quartered bananas and fry as you would doughnuts. Serve warm with the following sauce: Boil three-fourths pint sweet milk, beat the yolk of one egg and a level teaspoonful flour with sugar enough to make the sauce very sweet. When the milk boils, stir this into it and let it cool. Flavor to taste.

CHEESE STRAWS.

One-half pound of cheese grated, two tablespoonfuls flour and the yolk of two eggs. Season with salt and pepper. Mix thoroughly and roll in a thin sheet. Cut into tiny rings and strips. Bake, being careful not to burn, as they bake quickly. When ready to serve place three sticks in two rings.

CHESTNUTS.

Cover one quart chestnuts with stock. Add two tablespoonfuls sugar and a pinch of salt, cook until tender. Don't stir. Chestnuts should be quartered.

GELATINE.

One-half box of Cox's gelatine, enough cold water to cover it, let stand a moment, then add a pint or little more of boiling water, two cups sugar, flavoring to taste, turn in mold. Make custard of a pint of milk, three yolks, three tablespoonfuls sugar. When cool, add vanilla and stir in lightly, stiffly beaten whites of eggs.

JELLY.

One package gelatine, one pint cold water, let stand two hours, then pour over it one quart boiling water, one and one-half pound sugar, one pint wine, juice of three lemons; strain it twice through a canton flannel bag. Instead of wine use juice of four lemons, gratings of two.

MINCE MEAT.

Mix together one cup sugar, one cup chopped apple, one-half cup raisins seeded and chopped, one-half cup currants, one-fourth cup butter, one tablespoonful molasses, one tablespoonful boiled cider, one teaspoonful cinnamon, one-half teaspoonful cloves, one-half grated nutmeg, one saltspoonful mace and one teaspoonful salt. Add enough stock, in which meat has been cooked, to moisten; heat slowly to boiling point and let simmer an hour; then add one cup of chopped meat and two tablespoonfuls Barberry jelly. Cook fifteen minutes. If Barberry jelly is not to be obtained, use some other kind.

OATMEAL GRUEL FOR BABIES.

Boil for three hours or more two tablespoonfuls of oatmeal in one quart of water. Reduce liquid to one pint and strain. The long boiling is necessary to break down the cell walls and to make the gruel easy of digestion by the delicate stomach.

TOMATO SAUCE.

Put a tablespoonful butter and one of flour in a saucepan; mix until smooth, add one-half pint strained tomatoes, a bay leaf, one-fourth teaspoonful celery seed. Stir constantly until boiling; add one-half teaspoonful salt, one-quarter teaspoonful paprika. Strain and use.

WELSH RAREBIT.

One-fourth pound grated cheese, one-fourth cup cream or milk, one-half teaspoonful mustard, one-half teaspoonful salt, a little cayenne pepper, one egg, one teaspoonful butter, dry toast. Put cheese and milk or cream in double boiler, mix mustard, salt and cayenne; add egg and beat well. When cheese is melted, stir in mixture of dry ingredients and the egg, then the butter, and cook until it thickens. Stir constantly. Pour it over toast. Moderate heat and constant stirring, two important points.

YORKSHIRE PUDDING.

Beat the yolks of three eggs until light colored and thick; add one-half teaspoonful salt and one pint of milk. Add the mixture slowly to two-thirds cup flour, stir until smooth, then cut and fold in the white of eggs which have been beaten until stiff and dry. Bake in hot, well-greased gem pans forty-five minutes. Baste with drippings.

HELPFUL HINTS

Dredge your cake tins with flour and your cake will not stick to the pan.

Wooden spoons are the best to use when making cakes.

A little butter added to cake frosting greatly improves it.

Moisten grease spots with cold water and soda before scrubbing, as it lightens the task.

To polish hardwood floors, use equal parts of vinegar, turpentine and olive oil, thoroughly mixed: Rub in and polish with soft cloth.

To remove mildew stains, cover spots with lemon juice and salt and let dry in the sun.

Place a piece of wax paper over a knife when cutting butter.

If raisins and currants are rolled in flour before putting in a cake, they will not sink to the bottom.

When cutting fresh bread, have the knife very hot.

Put a pinch of salt in the whites of eggs to make them whip better.

Stains on knives, however obstinate, will disappear if rubbed with a piece of raw potato.

Put a slice of potato in the deep fat when frying doughnuts.

If potatoes are pared and laid in cold water just before boiling, they will be much whiter.

Rice will absorb three times its measure of water and a large quantity of milk or stock.

One ounce of butter equals two level tablespoonfuls.

One ounce of flour equals four tablespoonfuls.

Allow two level teaspoonfuls of baking powder to each cup of flour when no eggs are used.

A USEFUL TABLE.

Three teaspoonfuls equal one tablespoonful.
Four tablespoonfuls equal a quarter cup.
One cup of butter or sugar equals one-half pound.
Two cups of flour equals one-half pound.
One rounded tablespoonful of butter, one ounce.
One quart sifted pastry flour equals one pound.
One pint of granulated sugar equals one pound.
One pint of butter equals one pound.
One pint of ordinary liquid, one pound.

PROPORTIONS.

One teaspoonful baking powder to one cup flour.

One teaspoonful cream of tartar and one-half teaspoonful soda to two cups flour.

A little over an ounce of gelatine to a quart of liquid.

MILK.

Sour milk is used to raise doughs and batters, by adding to one pint solidly sour milk one teaspoonful soda. Mixtures which contain molasses require more soda.

BEVERAGES

"I drink to the general joy of the whole table."

CHOCOLATE.

Use one and one-half squares of bitter chocolate, one-fourth cup sugar, three cups milk, one cup boiling water and a few grains of salt. Scald the milk. Melt the chocolate in small saucepan, place over hot water, add sugar, salt, and gradually the boiling water. When smooth, place on the fire and boil for one minute; add to scalded milk, mill, and serve in chocolate cups with whipped cream. One and one-half ounces of vanilla chocolate may be substituted for the bitter; as it is sweetened, less sugar is needed.

CHOCOLATE.

German chocolate, three sticks in a boiler; let melt. Add one pint hot milk, let boil, then stir it for five minutes. Serve with whipped cream on top. Melt in double boiler.

COCOA.

One and one-half tablespoonfuls prepared cocoa, two tablespoonfuls sugar, two cups boiling water, two cups milk, and very little salt. Scald milk. Mix cocoa, sugar and salt, dilute with one-half cup boiling water to make smooth paste, add remaining water, and boil one minute; turn into scalded milk and beat two minutes with Dover egg beater until frothy.

COFFEE.

Use one tablespoonful of coffee to a cup, and one for the pot. Moisten with cold water and mix well with the white of egg. Make with boiling water and boil five minutes. Then let it stand in a hot place ten minutes. Do not simmer—merely keep hot.

COFFEE.

One cup ground coffee, seven cups cold water, one-fourth an egg. Scald granite-ware pot, dilute the egg with one-half cup of the cold water, stir into the coffee and mix thoroughly. Add the rest of the water and bring to a boil slowly. Remove to back of stove, add one tablespoonful of cold water, and allow it to stand a few minutes.

COMMITTEE JULEP.

Five lemons, two oranges, two cups water, one bunch fresh mint, three bottles ginger ale, one and one-half cup sugar; ice. Squeeze the juice from lemons and oranges, add leaves from mint, sugar and water. Let stand thirty minutes, add a large piece of ice and ginger ale. Serve in small glasses.

GRAPE JUICE.

Many people are not aware of the excellent qualities of this delightful and refreshing beverage. It is soothing to the nerves and aids the appetite. When prepared according to the recipe given below it makes a delicious and wholesome drink for persons in robust health, and in addition to this will prove beneficial to those of frail constitutions.

Stem grapes and put them into a kettle with enough water to show. Heat slowly, until grapes are soft enough to mash. Put them in a cheese-cloth bag, and when cool enough, press till every drop of juice is extracted. To two quarts of juice add one cup of sugar; heat and stir until sugar is thoroughly dissolved. Bottle, cork and seal. When serving this drink, dilute with water according to taste.

TEA.

Scald an earthen or china teapot. Use a teaspoonful of tea for each person and one for the pot. Put into the pot and pour in freshly boiled water, a cupful to each spoonful of tea. *Never boil tea*, but let it stand in a warm place a few minutes before serving. Serve with or without milk and sugar.

Tea and coffee, like all stimulants, should be used only in moderation. The use of either by children or dyspeptics is not to be recommended. Pure water is the best drink ordinarily for everybody. Most people prefer cold water, as it is not so insipid as boiled, but a cup of hot water taken in the morning on arising and one at night just before retiring will prove of benefit to sufferers from dyspepsia or indigestion.

THE FIRELESS COOKER.

The idea of the fireless cooker is an old one, bringing things to a boil, placing into a box of hay and leaving for a few hours to cook—that method has been used by housewives in some European nations for a good many years.

The cooker is, of course, made upon the same principle as that almost indispensable article, the refrigerator. Instead of retaining the cold and keeping out the heat, the fireless cooker does the opposite by keeping food which has been brought to a boiling point at a temperature high enough to continue the process of cooking for many hours.

Every one has wrapped up ice in a newspaper or carpet to keep it from melting. In making the fireless cooker the material used for packing around the boiling food is paper, hay, wool or cork, because any one of these things is a poor conductor of heat—that is, the heat can not go through them easily. Though there are many makes of fireless cookers on the market, a home-made one will serve the purpose just as well, and for the convenience afforded requires a comparatively small amount of time and material.

A HOME-MADE FIRELESS COOKER.

Materials required: A box or barrel, one pair of strong hinges, a hasp, material for stuffing, one or more large pails, one or more small pails or pans, muslin—1½ yard or more, depending on size of box; a cooking thermometer, heavy pasteboard, brown paper, tacks and screws.

The box selected may be an unpainted one, to be had from most any store for a few pennies, but the boards should be heavy enough to put on hinges and a hasp. It should be four or five inches larger than the kettle it is to contain. The easiest stuffings to procure are hay, excelsior, or paper; among others which should be covered to keep them in place are wool, mineral wool, cork, sawdust and cotton. If hay is used, it should be soft.

The best shape for the cooking utensil is a pail about the depth of its own diameter; the sides should be straight and perpendicular to the bottom, and the cover should fit securely in place. A smaller utensil may be used inside the larger one; a pudding pan serves the purpose, resting on the rim of the pail. Care should always be taken to have covers that fit snugly on any pans that are used in the cooker. Aluminum ware makes the best utensil, though enameled ware or agate ware may be used. A six-quart pail with a pan to fit inside of it is a good size for the ordinary family.

It is best to line the box and cover with a thickness of heavy paper or several thicknesses of newspaper; asbestos sheeting may be used instead of paper. Now pack in the box a firm layer of packing material about four inches deep, not less; this must raise the cooking pail to within three to five inches of top of box. Place utensil in middle of space on this layer and pack around it closely until level with top of the kettle. When it is removed a hole will be left just large enough for it to slip into again.

A cushion should be made to cover the kettle. If more than one kettle is used a cushion should be made for each. The cushion must be thick enough to fill the box when the kettle is in place. Cut two pieces of muslin or denim the sizes of top of box and join with a strip which is four or five inches wide; fill with same material used in packing the box. There should always be a slight pressure when the lid is closed.

The box is now ready for cooking. If the whole space is not firmly filled after considerable use, more stuffing should be added. If a covering is wanted for the stuffing, the simplest thing to use is a sheet of very heavy paper, at least one inch larger than the top of box; draw a circle in center of it the size of the pail. From center of circle cut with sharp scissors to edge, to strike it at intervals of about 1½ inch. Fit paper over top of packing so that circle will come just over nest for pail. Place pail in nest and it will crease the paper down at exactly the right place.

Since it is very important for the food to be placed into the cooker while it is still boiling, the box should be placed as near to the stove as possible. Everything should be ready before the food is taken from the fire; the cooker open and the cushion removed. The box must be kept tightly closed from the time the food is put in until it is entirely done. If it is necessary to open the box before appointed time, the contents must be reheated to the boiling point before it is replaced. Though the time necessary to cook the foods on the stove is very short, they must be boiled until heated to the center. Thus the denser and larger the food, the longer it will take to heat.

THE ADVANTAGES OF THE FIRELESS COOKER.

One of the advantages of the fireless cooker has been mentioned—the small amount of cooking over a fire, which means a great saving of fuel and attention. The housekeeper may put the food into the cooker and forget about it until meal time comes, busying herself in the meantime with other things, or perhaps leaving home. She knows that the food is not being ruined by burning, and that it will come to the table with its full flavor unimpaired.

The pails used in a fireless cooker are easier to clean than pans which have had the food burned into them, and the kitchen is never made a degree warmer by use of the cooker, which is certainly agreeable during the hot summer weather, and even onions may be cooked without the odor pervading the house.

Nearly all foods may be cooked in the fireless cooker except those which have to be crisp or brown, though roast meat may be browned either before placing in the cooker or when the process of cooking is nearly finished. Cereals, one of the most wholesome foods known, are greatly improved by use of the fireless cooker. The long cooking makes them more digestible and gives them a flavor which they lack when cooked only fifteen or twenty minutes.

Any person having a fair idea of the general principles of cooking will need very little instruction for the successful use of the fireless cooker. The following recipes do not pretend to cover the wide variety of food possible to fireless cookery, but only give an idea in the preparation of a few simple dishes that might be used for most any meal.

BEEF BROTH.

Wash one pound of lean beef from the shoulder or round. Chop the meat fine and remove pieces of fat; put meat into a pint of cold water with one-fourth teaspoon of salt and let it soak in a cold place for an hour. Place meat in a small cooker pan set over a large cooker pail of hot (but not boiling) water; heat the broth until it registers 165 degrees Fahrenheit. Slip pails into cooker for half an hour. Strain through coarse wire strainer, remove fat and serve at once in a heated cup. It may be chilled or frozen to the consistency of mush.

ROLLED OATS.

Remove any husks or pieces from one cup of rolled oats. Put two and a half cups of water, one teaspoon of salt and oats into a pan that fits into a cooker pail.

Boil until slightly thickened, stirring frequently; put pan over a cooker pail of boiling water and put into a cooker for from four to twelve hours. This is the ideal way to prepare rolled oats, as it is almost impossible to cook it too long.

BOILED POTATOES.

Scrub potatoes with a small brush. Pare them and let them stand a while in cold water. Cook them in a large amount of boiling salted water in a cooker pail. When they have boiled one minute put them in the cooker for from one and a half to three hours. New potatoes will not require so long to cook as old.

BOILED FISH.

Put a three-pound fish or three pounds of small fish into four quarts of boiling water to which four teaspoonfuls of salt have been added; set it at once into a cooker for one hour.

POT ROAST.

Have the butcher bone and roll three pounds of beef rump; dredge it well with salt, pepper and flour and brown it on all sides in a frying pan with a little of the fat from the meat. Put the meat, three cups of boiling water, one bay leaf, one small onion, salt and pepper, two small carrots, two sprigs parsley, one-half teaspoon celery seed, a little flour, one-half teaspoon Worcestershire sauce into a small cooker pail and let it simmer thirty minutes; set in a large pail of boiling water and put into a cooker for nine hours or more. Reheat it to boiling point; strain; thicken the liquor for gravy.

RICE PUDDING.

Heat one quart of milk, one teaspoonful of butter, one-third cup of rice, one-eighth teaspoon of grated nutmeg, one-eighth teaspoon of salt and one-half cup of sugar in a pudding pan over a cooker pail of water. When water boils remove pan and bring pudding also to a boil. When boiling, replace pudding in large pan of boiling water, cover and put into cooker for three or four hours. One-half cup of small unbroken seeded raisins may be added to this recipe, and the pudding may be browned in oven before serving, if desired.

STEWED CHICKEN.

Clean and cut up a chicken. Put it, with the giblets, in enough boiling salted water to cover it—one teaspoonful of salt to each quart of water. Let it boil for ten minutes and put it into a cooker for ten hours or more. If not quite tender, bring it again to a boil and cook it for six or eight hours, depending on its toughness. Skim off as much fat from the liquor as possible, pour off some of the liquor to use as soup or stock, and thicken the remainder with flour for gravy. A beaten egg or two stirred into the gravy just before serving improves it. Add pepper and salt to taste, and serve chicken on hot platter with gravy poured around it.

SETTING THE TABLE.

A most important thing necessary to the enjoyment of life, and an actual aid to digestion and the preservation of health, is that each person should make up his or her mind to forget all but pleasant thoughts and to put an absolute bar against the discussion of disagreeable subjects while at the table. Then only can they appreciate the fact that the meal has been carefully prepared and the table daintily set.

To cook an excellent meal and then serve it well makes the meal perfect. First of all the table linen should be immaculate. The more inexpensive linens are as attractive as the handsomest damasks when absolutely spotless and snowy white. For the lighter meals, breakfast and luncheon, a center piece and doilies may be used instead of the table cloth. The silver should be polished frequently and glasses wiped out carefully before placing on the table. A small fern or low bowl filled with short-stemmed flowers in the center of the table gives a dainty, cozy air, while the more elaborate vases may be used on more formal occasions. Four shaded candles on the table, when there are side lights in the dining room, cast a soft and pleasing light, far more agreeable to the eyes than the usual chandelier.

The placing of the silver must, of course, suit the character of the meal. If the meal is simple, the service should be simple. A good arrangement for an ordinary dinner is to place the fork and teaspoon at left of space allowed for plate, the knife and butter knife at the right, the napkin on right side and coffee spoon at the top, with water glass at the right and butter plate at left of each place. Various articles may be added, such as oyster fork, bouillon spoon, salad fork and so forth.

FOOD FOR, AND SERVING THE SICK.

The utmost care should be taken in cooking food for the invalid, so that all of the flavor and delicacy of each dish may be preserved. We take it for granted that the food is the best that can be had, and that absolute cleanliness is used in preparation. But, really, the important thing is to make the tray as attractive and dainty as possible, or the food will not be tempting, no matter how carefully prepared.

The tray should have a fresh, white cover each time it is carried to the sick room, and thin china of a pretty pattern should be used. In the summer time any garden flower, laid on the fresh napkin beside the plate, lends a cheerful note of color to the tray. Always serve small portions, as a large helping does not look appetizing to sick, tired eyes, and be careful in serving liquids not to spill any on the tray cloth or saucer.

It is those little things that sometimes disgust the invalid with what is put before him. There is a tidy and an untidy way of serving most dishes, too; for instance, in serving a poached egg, have it piping hot and on the toast; not cold, part on the toast and part on the saucer, with the yolk broken.

So each detail should be carried out, and you will find your care and attention rewarded by the invalid's interest in the tray, with its tinkling china and savory dishes.

Invalids should have graham bread, and must not be permitted to eat bread less than twenty-four hours old. Toast is a very good thing for most sick people, and should be browned very slowly in order that it may be dried through. It is then partially digested. It is best eaten dry.

Broths and soups are much used; oyster soup may be given, as well as gruel made of oatmeal or barley. Soups made of vegetables must be strained and served according to the doctor's orders.

Scraped beef is very nutritious, and is served raw between slices of bread and butter. Baked and broiled fish are nice, and generally relished by sick people.

Soft boiled and scrambled eggs are quite safe to give, as a rule.

If potatoes are liked, have them baked. Other vegetables may be given, but it is always best to consult the physician before serving things about which one is doubtful. Food that will not be harmful in some cases may be decidedly so in others. Generally, it is best to avoid fried and warmed-over meats, and pork should not be served to the sick.

Avoid unripe or overripe fruit. In serving oranges, remove the tough part and give only the juice. Baked and stewed apples are to be recommended; sometimes baked custard, and rice or other puddings. If any stewed berries are to be used, be sure to strain them.

Coffee is good to use moderately in malarial troubles, and tea, not very strong, may be used sparingly when the heart is not affected. Milk, when it agrees with the patient, may be given. Lemonade and lemon water ice are very refreshing and will often be taken when other drinks do not seem tempting.

DEFINITIONS OF SOME FOREIGN AND OTHER TERMS.

Á la, au, aux. With or dressed in a certain style.

Allemande (à la). In German style.

Americaine (à la). In American style.

Asperges. Asparagus.

Au gratin. With browned crumbs.

Bannocks. Scotch cakes made of barley or oatmeal.

Basil. A pot herb.

Bay leaves. Leaves from a species of laurel.

Bearnaise (à la). In Swiss style.

Bèchamel (à la). With sauce made of chicken stock and milk or cream.

Beignet. Fritter.

Beurre noir. Black butter.

Biscuit glace. Small cakes of ice cream.

Bisque. A soup, generally made of shell fish; or an ice cream to which is added finely chopped nuts.

Blanch (to). To whiten.

Boeuf braisé. Braised beef.

Boeuf à la jardiniere. Braised beef with vegetables.

Bouchées. Mouthful. Small patties.

Bouquet of herbs. A sprig each of thyme, savory, marjoram and parsley.

Bourgeoise (à la). In family style.

Café noir. Black coffee.

Chartreuse. A mould of aspic in which there are vegetables; something concealed.

Chaud-froid. Literally, hot cold. A jellied sauce.

Chou-fleur. Cauliflower.

Chutney. A sweet pickle from East India.

Civet. A game stew.

Compotes. Fruits stewed in syrup and kept in their original shape.

Consommé de volaille. Chicken soup.

Créole (à la). With tomatoes.

Curry powder. A yellow powder containing tumeric.

De, d'. Of.

Écossaise (à l'). In Scottish style.

En papillotes. In papers.

Entrée. A dish served to introduce the main part of the dinner.

Farci-e. Stuffed.

Fillet de boeuf piqué. Larded fillet of beef.

Flammande (à la). In Holland style.

Fondue. A dish made of cheese and eggs.

Fraises. Strawberries.

Frappeé. Generally whipped and semi-frozen.

Fricassée de poulet. Fricasse of chicken.

Fromage. Cheese.

Gateau. Cake.

Gelée. Jelly.

Grilled. Broiled.

Hachis de boeuf. Beef hash.

Hors-d'oeuvres. Side dishes.

Huitres en coquille. Oysters in the shell.

Italienne (à la). In Italian style.

Jambon froid. Cold ham.

Kirschwasser. Liquor made from cherry juice.

Kuchen. German for cake.

Kümmel. Liquor flavored with cumin and caraway seed.

Lait. Milk.

Laitue. Lettuce.

Macaroni au fromage. Macaroni with cheese.

Maigre. A vegetable soup without stock.

Maître d'hotel. Head steward.

Mango. A fruit of the West Indies, Mexico and Florida.

Maraschino. A cordial.

Marrons. Chestnuts.

Menu. Bill of fare.

Noir. Black.

Nouilles. Noodles.

Oeufs pochés. Poached eggs.

Omelette aux fine herbes. Omelet with fine herbs.

Omelette aux champignons. Omelet with mushrooms.

Pain. Bread.

Panade. Bread and milk cooked to a paste.

Paté de biftecks. Beefsteak pie.

Paté de fois gras. A paste made of fatted geese livers.

Pois. Peas.

Pommes. Apples.

Pommes de terre. Potatoes.

Potage. Soup.

Polets sautés. Fried chicken.

Queues de boeuf. Ox tails.

Ragoût. A highly seasoned meat dish.

Réchauffes. Warmed-over dishes.

Removes. The roasts or principal dishes.

Ris de veau. Sweetbreads.

Salade de legumes. Vegetable salad.

Salpicon. Highly seasoned minced meat mixed with a thick syrup

Soufflé. Puffed up.

Soup a l'ognon. Onion soup.

Sucres. Sweets.

Tarte aux pommes. Apple pie.

Tourte. A tart.

INDEX

D

E

F

H

P

Q

R

W

Y

Lector House believes that a society develops through a two-fold approach of continuous learning and adaptation, which is derived from the study of classic literary works spread across the historic timeline of literature records. Therefore, we aim at reviving, repairing and redeveloping all those inaccessible or damaged but historically as well as culturally important literature across subjects so that the future generations may have an opportunity to study and learn from past works to embark upon a journey of creating a better future.

This book is a result of an effort made by Lector House towards making a contribution to the preservation and repair of original ancient works which might hold historical significance to the approach of continuous learning across subjects.

HAPPY READING & LEARNING!

LECTOR HOUSE LLP
E-MAIL: lectorpublishing@gmail.com

9 789389 614190